I Don't Have My Decision Making Trousers On

by John J Bowen

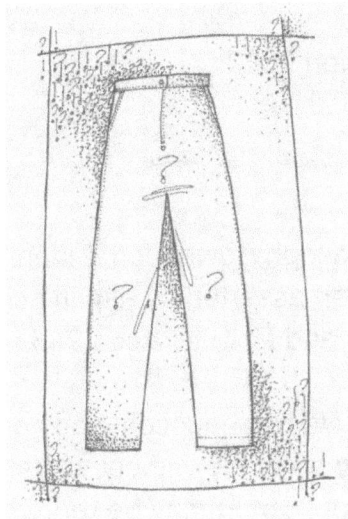

Copyright

I Don't Have My Decision Making Trousers On is published by Gulfhaven Ltd

2nd edition, February 2012. First published on Kindle in December 2011

The Legal Stuff

For Clarity

There are a lot of talented John Bowens out there, several of whom have written books, plays, screenplays and more. I merely share their name, and apologise to them if anyone mistakes them for me, or vice versa, and so for the purposes of my business writing you will often find me billed as John J Bowen, and in many other columns and blogs I use the tag line:

John Bowen
is

That Consultant Bloke

The story of That Consultant Bloke appears at the end of this book.

Other Writing

You will find my Monday Musings blog at
http://thatconsultantbloke.wordpress.com/

I write for a number of magazines in various sectors and contributed two chapters for The Principles of Warehouse Design, 3rd Edition edited by Dr Peter Baker and published by the Chartered Institute of Logistics & Transport ISBN 978-1904564324

Social Media
You can follow my Tweets @bowenjohnj
Connect with me on LinkedIn
http://uk.linkedin.com/in/johnjbowen

Dedication

For Fay, sometimes referred to in these stories as The
Wokingham Wonder or The Berkshire Belle
Thanks and love also to Stephanie in Far North Queensland,
Australia, for the trousers artwork. Find out more about her art
and activities at www.stephaniejmilne.com

Contents

Introduction

I am a very lucky man. I was brought up in a decent home by decent people and, whilst we moved around a lot, I lived in some wonderful places.

My education may have been the basic United Kingdom primary and secondary one of the late 1950s and 1960s that is so derided today, but I learned what I was taught and I think that they taught me well despite racking up 5 different schools in the 12 years that I attended.

I showed my first entrepreneurial flair at the age of 5 growing and selling lettuce, started work in what we would now call logistics (I was the village butcher's boy) at 11, began driving for a living at 13 (on the farm) and took my first managerial role at 14 running the school library.

From that promising start I loused things up somewhat. I failed to get the top grades in any of my formal exams, took two goes to pass my driving test and did nothing to sort out a proper career until nearly three years after leaving school. Even then I casually threw away the golden opportunity that I had been handed.

I got myself back on track, bought a house, got married, started a family and knuckled down. A second addition to the family arrived, hard work paid off by creating another chance and a happy accident landed me in the spotlight. My charge up the greasy pole of management was under way, but as I went up my marriage went down and, despite a fight, we parted after 12 years,

Happily for me I met the Berkshire Belle and we have been together for 22 years now. I got far enough up that greasy pole to enjoy the fruits and trappings, but every step took me further from the action and so I resigned.

At that stage I had just come through my own Blackest Day. I left the rooms of an oral consultant having been told that the swelling in the roof of my mouth was a tumour that needed to be urgently removed so that they could decide whether or not I had further problems, but I had to face, as a minimum, that my ability to communicate vocally could be changed for good. As I walked back to my car I switched on my cell phone. It told me I had messages, one of which was an urgent summons to the hospital where my Mother was dying. She slipped quietly away an hour later. By one of those strange co-incidences my newest grand-daughter Sabina was born in the same hospital around 12 hours later.

And so I set out on my own just 6 months before the financial world dissolved around us all, but I have not looked back. The last three and a half years have been a wonderful mixture of projects and assignments. Four operations have interrupted that period, but I am clear and free of Larry the Lump and in generally rude health for a 59 year old who still thinks that he is 19.

I am a very lucky man and the following pages share some of my experiences and thoughts. I've grouped them into loose headings as chapters and I hope that they provoke you to think about yourself, your work and your place in the world. If just one helps you then this was a book worth writing.

Prologue

He stood for a moment before the office door. A tall, gangling and spotty young man dressed in a dust stained warehouse coat. At one end of him black and white baseball boots peeked from beneath the red velvet bell bottom trousers and at the other end a mop of wavy brown hair sprang from a centre parting to cloak his shoulders.

No-one had told him why he was summoned to see the boss. He was at the end of his fifth week at the firm, his probationary week having proved satisfactory he had been told that he was on an eight week trial, but there had been a few, well issues, so was his trial about to end? Only one way to find out, so he straightened his back, took a pace forward and knocked. Barely two minutes later he walked from the office closing the door behind him. As he walked back to his work area he little knew that those steps were the start of a management journey. Far from being sacked he had been told that, despite not having the required educational qualifications, he was being placed on the management training scheme. They had seen some potential.

That gangling, spotty youth was me, and I look back over the not quite 40 years since that day with a great deal of gratitude. The spark that they saw and tried to fan took a while to burst into flame, but it eventually did so because of their taking the time to invest in me.

Over the years I've tried to pay back that debt by helping others. I've built some great teams and I've had some failures, but I have a huge pride in the people that have come through my teams and gone on to greater things.

In the pages that follow you'll find out about some of the things that have succeeded and failed for me over time. I hope that these thoughts and stories will help you too. If they do, perhaps you can pass them on to others in turn.

ThatConsultantBloke
November 2011

Chapter One - Right Reasons

Doing the right thing, or acting for the right reasons, is what makes a good leader stand out. Their people and their stakeholders will trust them and believe in them if they can see that things are being done for the right reasons, even if they may not agree.

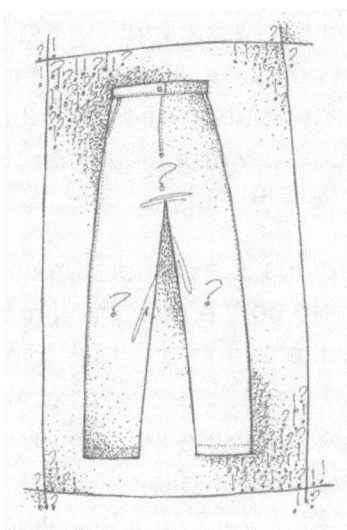

Why are you bothering? No-one else does

The Berkshire Belle says this to me quite often. When I park the car properly, when I go out in the pouring rain to get to the post box before the last collection, when I hold the door for someone who ignores me and just sweeps through. There are all sorts of occasions. It came up again one Sunday when I went out to drop off some papers for someone who needed help even though I could have spent the time productively on something that I wanted to do. So why do I bother?

Most of it is rooted in my upbringing. I was given values by my parents, my teachers and the other adults who influenced me. Being taught what was right and what was wrong. Yes I have strayed over the years; I'm nowhere near perfect, but I do have that basic set of behaviours and I try to live up to them. So I park the car properly so as not to inconvenience anyone else. If I've promised to mail something today I will, even if I get wet going to the post box, and when a friend asks if I can help them out with some information that they need today, I'll do what I can, if necessary dropping what I'm doing to help them. It's the way I was brought up and it's who I am.

Being true to your values is a cornerstone of leadership. You have to be prepared to do the right thing regardless of personal cost. Over the years I've stuck to my guns even when, as we used to say at one place I worked, such actions could be career inhibiting. Sure it can hurt you in the short term, but the longer term benefits are worth it in terms of self-esteem and, as a leader, your people will be far more prepared to follow you if they can believe in you as someone that they can trust to do the right thing.

So how do I feel about those that don't live by my standards? What they do is their business. If we are talking about people that I work with, then I try to lead by example, but the degree of influence I can have on the world at large is very limited so, as The Wokingham Wonder asks, why do I bother?

I bother because I want to. I bother because if I don't I let down the people who took the trouble to bring me up the right way. I let down the people who believe in me and I let myself down. Why should I lower my standards just because others behave badly? It might be easier, but that doesn't make it right.

As leaders we have to set standards, and it is more and more necessary in a world where standards are falling: The disgraceful behaviour of our politicians over their expenses displays a lack of leadership that staggers me. In the business world it is gross misconduct and the penalty should be instant dismissal, but they stole public money and got away with it. What sort of example are they setting?

In the face of things, maintaining standards may not seem worth bothering with, but I am not prepared to give up. Even if I am the last one standing up for what I believe in I will stay on my feet. Call me old fashioned. Call me a dinosaur. Call me what you like (sticks and stones etc), but I do not want to change and do not intend to. I bother because I care, and that's good enough for me.

Right or wrong are you prepared to make a decision?

Right or wrong? I've written in my blog several times on the theme of leaders doing what is right, people doing the right thing and so on, but what is right and what is wrong? Surely, if I have been right in some of my earlier musings leaders will know these things? Or was I wrong?

We tend to think of right and wrong in absolute terms, but they are not always absolutes. It was cooking that got me onto this train of thought; in baking, say cakes or bread, you are into chemical reactions, so the ratio between quantities of ingredients is critical to get the recipe to work as are timings for resting, proving or cooking, and you need to get things right or the result will probably end up in the trash. But if you are making, say, a stew, you can put in all sorts of things and still end up with an edible meal.

So what has this to do with leaders being right or wrong in their business decisions? We have to make decisions, but the measure of right and wrong is often nebulous. We are judged on success, but would we have been more or less successful if our decision had been different? As long as the results are good, probably we don't care. Yes, we may do a post implementation review on projects or bids, but how much of the outcome of that do we plough back into our decision making process? Do we actually have a decision making process? Lots of companies I've worked with and for don't, but I do myself, even if it does make me feel a bit of an anorak at times.

Here's another angle. If I make the decision to close an operating division, am I right or wrong? This one is hugely affected by the impact it has on the individual. If you are a shareholder and my action helps the dividend, then I was right. The CEO and other senior executives will also probably say I was right, but their personal gain from profit related bonuses will also help their perception. But if you are one of the redundant workers, or a supplier who has lost a contract or a local retailer that the workers used to spend their wages with you may well have a different view. So was I right to shut the operation or was I wrong?

Is the measure here in terms of the majority? After all, for society to work we have the democratic principle of majority decision. For a leader or manager you can be open to accusations of self-interest, but I would counter that from a personal view by pointing out that I've more than once instigated a company restructure that has done away with my own job (and without a golden parachute).

As leaders we have to be decisive, so we need to be sure in our own minds that the decisions we have come to are the best that we can make. Sometimes these are the moments when leadership can be a very lonely place, and your courage is tested. This is where having some form of decision making process gives strength; you know that the decision you have made is as right as it can be under the prevailing circumstances.

Of course hindsight may show things differently, but anyone can make the right decision after the event. Real leaders are prepared to stand and be counted. They will admit to their mistakes and learn from them. They'll get it right more often than wrong.

Personal responsibility: Where did it go?

I'll try and keep this from turning into a rant, and I don't want to upset all my Health & Safety friends and colleagues either, but I do get concerns about the loss of personal responsibility in general life, especially as enshrined in the ever growing roll of legislation.

FM Guru Martin Pickard kicked me off on to this train of thought with one of his blogs about background checks, but I am talking here about a bigger picture: Why should someone be protected by law to the extent that they now are when they do something dumb? I was having a laugh with a colleague about a report of a thief who had broken into a site in the small hours, but had failed in his getaway when he hurt his back carrying the swag out. We joked that there was probably a case against the property owner for not having provided a risk assessment and lifting & handling training. Black humour, but too close for comfort these days.

Feel free to point out that I am an old fogey who's just banging on about "It wasn't like that in my day etc" if you want to, but it seems to me that we have lost any sense of people taking responsibility for their own actions.

This comes down to a leadership issue for me. As a leader you have to be prepared to accept responsibility. Your decisions need to be as good as they can be and you need to be prepared to accept the consequences of getting it wrong. Making mistakes is a fundamental part of learning (as I've said elsewhere in this book), but good leaders understand this and are prepared also to admit that they got it wrong and put things right before too much damage is done.

For some years now we have elected politicians who have no concept of leadership and most of whom are, in my opinion, cowards. Recent scandals in the UK over expenses alone indicate a both lack of leadership and of courage, but did they set the tone or just mirror it? I don't know. What I would like to see is folks in general having the guts to stand on their own two feet and to stop trying to blame someone else when things go wrong. Life isn't fair; it's not supposed to be, so just get on and make the best of it.

In business, I see too many cases where people are failing to take personal responsibility for delivering results. All too often a good enough strategy fails because no-one actually steps up to the plate and makes things happen. I hear senior people tell me that, yes things will happen because they've told so and so to do it, quite often adding "or else". So it's the other person's fault when nothing happens? Wrong. The leader is responsible for making sure that things happen. They should be checking, without micro managing, and, where necessary helping and supporting the subordinate if they are struggling.

If getting it wrong means getting the sack, then that's the way it is. If I'd screwed up that badly I'd probably resign anyway, not that it makes much difference. It's about being responsible, so admit it was your fault.

Personal responsibility - it's a cornerstone of good leadership. It's one of the key factors in building the trust that leaders need. My challenge to you is to look at how you approach this - I'll be taking another look at my own behaviour.

Are you a Thinker or a Doer?

"Are you and thinker or a doer?" The questioner's piercing blue eyes gleamed at me despite the way he and his fellow interview panel members had placed themselves against the late afternoon sun (this was 30 or so years ago when people thought that this sort of thing was clever).

I said I was a doer and gave some examples, but this was clearly the wrong answer at the time. No, I didn't get the appointment, and I can't remember what the job was now, but I do still remember the question. So why did it matter then, and does it make any difference to my style of leadership?

Looking back to that time I'd say that I was a doer who did think a bit about what he was doing. My focus was almost never at a micro level, just about the current or next issue rather than on a wider scale, but focused on getting the job done. Maybe this was more a tactical approach rather than strategic, but always with an eye on delivering the strategy.

I had arrived in a senior management position in this big organisation less than 8 years after joining on the shop floor, and barely five years after my first management role there, although I had been a manager in previous companies. That interview question bothered me though: If I was to progress, should I try to change or to be something else? What should I change and how?

Life goes on and this encounter got pushed to the back of my mind, but it came back to me recently and got me thinking again. I did progress further up the ladder at that company, and did become very strategic, but my reputation, and therefore the promotions, was always results based. A couple of companies later and further up the greasy pole I resigned because I'd got to a level where I didn't feel that I was actually doing very much at all. My role was one where I'd think and discuss and plan and review, but it was always someone else who did the doing, and the organisational structure took away any influence on whether or not they really did do it (often they didn't). So I left and found myself a role where I can both think and do and am happily making things happen again.

Looking back at close to 40 years of full time working life I would say that I'm a doer who has been successful because I think about what I do.

So are you a thinker or a doer? How do you see yourself and what do I suggest you do?

My advice to younger folks making their way in life and business is that you should do what you're good at, be satisfied with that, but don't stop learning and adapting to get better at doing it. And don't worry about trying to be something that you aren't, just get comfortable with who you are and what you do, and strive to be the best at it that you can be.

Be true to yourself and do things honestly. The world needs thinkers and doers and there is plenty of room for both. There is no shame in being one or the other and, as a leader, I'm always grateful for both on my teams; I need people who can think and plan and people who can take those plans and make them happen. My role is to make sure that, between us all, the results do get delivered and I'll try to build the team and the individuals along the way. It's what I do.

Education Yesterday and Today

I read regularly that the education techniques used in the 1950s and 1960s have been discredited. Now I am a product of that system, starting school in 1956 and leaving in 1969. I can write and spell reasonably, and can still do a decent range of sums without resort to a calculator. I remember sizeable chunks of what I was taught in lessons such as history, geography, biology, music, woodwork, metalwork, art, music and apply elements of all that I learned on a daily basis.

The reason for this train of thought is twofold; firstly that a revised edition of a standard textbook has just been published and it contains two chapters written by me.

Secondly, my complimentary copy of that book arrived on a day that I had just spend working with others on preparing examination marking frameworks and setting problems for students taking examinations at first degree level, part of an on-going project for me working for one of the UKs leading professional bodies.

Now these contributions to the academic world are hardly earth shattering, but I was reflecting on how my school teachers might feel to know that one of their former pupils had gone on to play his own small part in the learning machine when I read on LinkedIn yet another posting about how poor education was 40 years ago and how much it has advanced to the present day.

If that is true, why am I seeing job applications from university graduates who cannot spell or punctuate? Why am I working with graduates who have no idea of the UKs geography let alone Europe or the world? Why am I looking at spreadsheets produced by graduates where there are elementary errors in the calculations that are not apparent to them from the results? I could go on, but let's just leave the list there.

I started at primary schools then on to county secondary modern schools, leaving at the age of 16. I did do some self-funded further education at night school, and some work funded education that led to various professional qualifications, one of which was ranked equivalent to a bachelor's degree when I was accepted to do a work funded MSc (which I didn't do in the end because business needs got in the way). Because my family moved around a lot I went to 3 different primary and 2 secondary schools. Five schools in twelve years may not have been ideal for a stable education, but the teachers at these gave me a good platform to work on from the curriculum subjects, and also in the extracurricular things that they put on in their own time.

So I say to those who cast aspersions about the way those good people taught that maybe you have it wrong: I think that we were well taught by good people.

Yes there were one or two who were maybe not so good, but they all cared about what they were doing and about those in their charge. I am grateful to what they taught me in lessons, outside of lessons and about life in general.

We all left school with the basics. What we did later may have been largely down to our own efforts and, for me, a lot of luck, but we were better equipped that most of the youngsters I've encountered as an employer over the last 30 years, and more so with those recently.

I don't suppose that any of those that taught me will ever be aware of what I'm up to these days, but thanks for everything.

P B Denny 1917 – 2009, A Quiet Inspiration

I learned recently that Peter Denny had died aged 92. He is one of my great inspirations, and his passing started me thinking about him, and of others who, knowingly or not, helped turn me into someone who can make things happen.

I talk about myself as someone who makes things happen. It is one of my passions, but it probably comes from a joy I had discovered in childhood; just making things. I built my first Airfix (plastic model) kit at 5 and went on to build all sorts of things, encouraged later on the practical side by my metalwork teacher Mr Baines, my biology teacher, Mr Dingle and one of my maths teachers, Mr Donovan reminded me of what I'd been taught about angles and calculations. To conceive, design, build and operate something gave me a huge thrill and started me on the road to now with some engineering basics.

My next lessons came from Peter Hopkins and James Patrick (Pat) Lee. They were my two managers, at different companies, during the mid 70s. They each taught me about delegation and teamwork and process, about how our small outposts fitted into the larger corporation, The System.

Later in life I was selected to train as a computer programmer/analyst working in a language called COBOL, then the industry standard for business applications. There Diane Santos taught me about applying discipline in my approach, reinforcing the engineering basics from school on a grander scale, and John Robson taught me to let my imagination fly, how to look at where you could go from here, but then where next, and next again. But both taught me, from opposite directions, how to use knowledge, experience, technology and people to get from here to what you dreamed about.

The pace of change in my lifetime has been huge. Mobile (cell) phones are far better than the personal communicators of science fiction in my childhood. In 1982 I was writing business applications to run on mainframes overnight and use no more than 1K of processing power. It took less than 70 years from the first manned, powered flight to landing men on the moon. All of these things have come because we can dream and have the people who can make those dreams happen, and I thank everyone who has showed me how that I, in my own way, can also make things happen.

So where does Peter Bond Denny fit into all of this? He was a man who made things and that is how I came to know him. He built what is probably the greatest model railway in the world, making virtually all of it from scratch and he built it with astonishing accuracy in terms of detail and prototype practice.

Everything worked as it did on the full size railway; signals, bell codes and operating practice. When his eldest son Crispin went off to university he designed and built a computer, the Automatic Crispin, to operate the other end of the layout (and this long before the PC was a twinkle in IBM's eye).

He wrote over 60 books and countless articles, which is where I encountered him, as well as building and re-building his layout and the models upon it. He started all of this during WW2 when materials were almost non-existent and did it all as a hobby whilst serving as a parish priest. He showed me that imagination and application can defeat all odds and his influence runs right through everything I try to do today. From a distance, Reverend Peter Denny, your quiet and humble inspiration made a difference. RIP.

You Can Turn a Wrong Into a Right

Many years ago I ran a big site. We had a security incident that resulted in us finally being given the budget to take security seriously, and I brought in expert help to plan a series of integrated systems and processes that we carefully implemented. To test these, without telling anyone, I hired a team to try and crack our new defences. They barely made a dent and we patted ourselves on the back and tightened up the area where they had made a slight inroad.

Over the following months we fended off a number of attempts to intrude, mostly innocent, but one very malicious. Then one evening I got a call to say that we had caught someone at the heart of the site and that the Police had been called to take over. I raced in myself and found that we had caught a 15 year old youth.
I called off the Police and let him go. He wouldn't talk, but we knew who he was and where he lived. It took us a few days, but study of CCTV recordings and a little common sense showed a gaping hole in our expensive defences. We had had a fundamental flaw right from the start, but our belief in the system had led us into a classic trap, so we learned a good lesson and made the necessary changes.

There was little we could do at the time in terms of tangible thanks to our juvenile intruder, but 18 months or so later when he turned 17 we gave him a job, trained and developed him and saw him move on to better things elsewhere. A better reward that the criminal record he might have got had we not called off the Police. I see him occasionally around town with his family, and his son must be nearly 15 years old himself now.

So where is the leadership lesson here? It would have been easy to lash out and seek retribution against the lad who had triggered this incident, but for what purpose other than to blame someone else? But I'd like to think that the lesson is in the fact that I took the failure on the chin: No recriminations, especially against the easy target of the youthful perpetrator, but acceptance that he had shown me that I had a problem in a relatively benign manner. Imagine the consequences if it had of been a malicious gang who had found the hole in my defences.

This is a true story. I was moved to include it here for a specific reason: It reminds me of another case, that of Gary McKinnon.

A Rose by Any Other Name?

Is there really anything new under the sun? Well of course there is; we live in an age where technology is moving as fast, if not faster, that at any time in our history.

I can remember, as a schoolboy, looking up at the moon and marvelling at how we had gone from the first powered flight to landing on the moon in just 66 years. I am now less than 10 years from that age, but in my time I have seen the pocket communicators that were a feature of Star Trek become a reality in the form of flip phones that are themselves now passé.

So what has sparked me off on this train of thought? Well I've been reminded of just how business life goes in circles. We centralise, then we decentralise and so on. Every time we do it for a good reason, but these pendulum swings can't always be right, can they?

I'll return to that in a moment because there is another side to this issue. It's one thing for us to decide to go back to doing things the way we were doing them 5 or 10 years ago, even if the past does get lost sometimes (all we learn from history is that we learn nothing from history), but I do get kind of niggled when these cycles are dressed up as The Next Big Thing. This approach smacks of the Emperor's New Clothes to me. If the right hype is applied, no-one is prepared to argue are they? Take TV shows for example. We're starting to hear the expression imported from the US "All new". Well that's just nonsense because it will be the same old cast for a start, and probably the same old set and writers as well, but it just gets accepted.

And the same is true in business. You can dress old stuff up as new and there will be people who will lap it up and, once they have bought into it, they won't be prepared to acknowledge the facts because they fear that they will look silly; "look at the stitching on those new clothes".

One of my major pieces of work at the moment is a purchasing consultancy. I am, in the jargon of the time, deep into category management. Now this has being dressed up as the way to do it for a while, but it is not really any different to what we called product management 20 odd years ago. We do have some powerful new tools to deploy; communication and the internet make a massive difference, but is the approach really that different? I think that we are really just doing the same things and calling them by a new name, and suggest that we are doing that because it makes it look like we are better and to help justify our existence.

Back at the swinging pendulum, I see the problem as being one of extremes. You head off in, say, the direction of decentralisation. Give power back to the people, devolve authority and chuck out the corporate manual. And yes, you get faster reactions and all sorts of good things but, if you don't control it you get corporate anarchy. And so the answer is to tighten, but rather than just a turn of the spanner, it all gets wound back in until the creativity is stifled and the cycle starts again.

Yes we need change and to adapt and evolve, and progress comes not from hype and snake oil salesmen, but from balance and keeping things in perspective.

Chapter Two – Leadership Lessons

I have my own style of leadership that has developed over time. In this chapter I share a few stories and thoughts on things that have helped me develop that style.

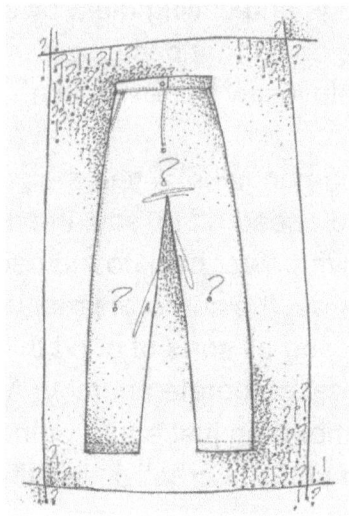

Friction is Good

Much of what we do as leaders is about maintaining harmony; good relations within and without the team make for happy people. Friction within the team is usually viewed as a bad thing, and most leadership thinking is about eliminating it.

But have you ever thought about why and how a wheel works? It has to have some grip on the surface or it won't turn - try driving on ice! We tend to talk about it as grip, but get technical and you're into friction co-efficients.

So friction is good - it causes forward motion, right?

Friction within your team is often destructive though so, as a leader, you need to exercise control. In the same way as you do as a driver in your car you have to manage the friction so that your tyres (tires) grip the surface and stop you disappearing into the scenery.

Managing friction is about allowing new ideas and thinking get into your team and controlling the debate so that these ideas get developed. It's about allowing people to disagree without falling out, and it's about getting good decisions made because you've thoroughly aired the topic.

When I talk about controlling the debate I mean ensuring that everyone is contributing; sometimes the friction element is about one or more of the team simmering and not contributing. You have to draw out their issues as much as you have to deal with the vociferous elements.

Being able to accept having your thinking challenged is a leadership trait. Encourage debate; the right answer is better than nodding heads.

Using friction well is actually a very powerful tool and great leaders understand the benefits it can bring.

Would you take piano lessons from someone who had never played?

One of the problems with leadership thinking is that a lot of what is currently being put around comes from people who have studied the subject, but who have never really done it themselves. Would you take golf lessons from someone who had never played a competitive round? Or someone who had bought a set of clubs and a video and taught themselves the rudiments? Hopefully not.

This difference gets further amplified when someone who has been shown how to do something gets to try and do it. Take a musical instrument; lots of people can get a tune out of one, but how many can really play one? Does someone who does a decent karaoke turn make a good singer? I can drive a car, but whilst we share the same initials, I'm no Jensen Button.

What makes the difference is talent. Good leaders can take the tools and use them to best effect in the same way that any virtuoso does with an instrument.

Most of these self-styled leadership experts put across a one size fits all solution which, if you think about it, is fundamentally flawed. Leadership is about leading people. People is plural; it refers to a group of individuals. And that is the key word; individuals.

People are different, and this leads to a real dichotomy for leaders. On the one hand current social thinking is that you should treat everyone equally, but how do you do that when everyone has different needs?

Leadership involves a range of techniques to motivate people according to their own needs. I don't respond well to people getting angry with me; One of the most effective things ever said to me when I screwed up badly was a very quiet "Bowen, you've let us all down. You've let me down, but, most of all, you've let yourself down". Some people would treat that with contempt though, but the guy who delivered it knew the difference; there were others on the team who, in similar circumstances, would have been blasted against the wall by a withering stream of invective, but he knew me well enough to know that that would not work on me.

That leader didn't deliberately set out to teach me how to do it, but the example was there for any of us to follow and adapt for our own use. And I did.

A good leader will know what makes each member of the team tick and will apply the right techniques, but then there is the question of what to do when you face the team all at once. Gung ho speeches don't do anything for me, but I've seen firsthand how they can get a team going, and there is a synergy factor that comes into play in those situations, but you have to get it right and catch the mood. No-one can teach you that. It's about working an audience and you learn by doing (and getting it wrong a few times).

A potentially good leader will have latent talent that can be developed. They then need the opportunity to lead and, for those who get the chance, they have the opportunity to hone their skills. Not all will make it, but it's better to have tried and failed.

Good leaders don't necessarily make good teachers, (but someone that teaches classes successfully will be a good leader). If you want to learn about leadership you first have to have the opportunity to do it. If you want help in learning, you need someone who can pass on to you the benefit of their experience.

We all need to keep learning, but, as in life in general, there are no quick and easy solutions to getting to be good at something.

Climbing the Greasy Pole

I was talking to a fellow consultant and we were sharing some of our experiences on climbing the greasy pole that is a feature of corporate life. About the same age, we'd both got to similar levels even if the routes we took were different, and that conversation got me thinking about some of the things I'd got wrong and right along my own journey.

When I left school back in 1969 I had passed my Civil Service entrance exam, but had been allocated a job at the courts in a North London borough. Living out in the sticks well to the South of the metropolis I couldn't get there in time to start work in the morning and enquiries about digs revealed prices that would have eaten away all of my pay. I had to decline and didn't get a second offer.

It took me about 3 years to get my act together and, despite the lack of relevant qualifications, the wholesaler I was working for put me on to their management training scheme. My first supervisory role involved being in charge of four women; two worked mornings and the other two the afternoons. Let's just say that it was a salutary lesson and quickly move on. I certainly did, but I had made a start, and I had three or four managers there who really worked on me. I didn't really appreciate what they did until later, but it did penetrate and so, also subconsciously, did the bad examples.

My opinion of myself outgrew reality though, and I moved on in search of new pastures, making a big mistake in doing so, but the next step saw me back amongst safe hands, and ones who again could see a spark of something.

Their efforts helped me see some of the benefit of what had gone before and I began to take tentative steps back into management with spells of relief manager duties at retail outlets and this time round I didn't screw up.

Marriage meant a change of scene and saw me back at the bottom of the heap again, but now watching management with a more critical eye. The big lesson learned here was more about how the corporate machine worked and this readied me for the next move which saw me off to head office in London with a promotion to a junior manager role as a computer programmer.

That first step is probably the hardest, and to make it into the cynical world of the big city turned it into a major one. Things worked well in many ways, but it was here that I had a road to Damascus moment when I actually heard myself one day and realised what a pompous pratt I had become. That revelation probably saved me.

No longer taking myself so seriously I used what I had learned about how the business worked to get onto a fast track up several rungs of the promotion ladder and, all of a sudden, twenty five years had gone by and I found myself stifled by a business that didn't know what to do with me so I walked out: Now I'm enjoying life again.

So what can I pass on? Well the first advice I can give is to keep your eyes and ears open and find out how things work. That the bosses like people with solutions, not problems was an early lesson, and being able to make things happen is what I built a career on in the end. The second piece of advice is from one Winston Churchill: "Never, never, never give up".

Final thought – stay humble.

What shape is leadership?

Take one of my clients. They are in the B2C sector and are growing fast. Back in 2009 we helped them bring some order to their leadership through strengthening their management team with some new people. Growth accelerated, despite the recession, and things look good for them, but they are at that stage where a fresh challenge has come. The issue is around structure. You need to have a framework to operate within, but also want to retain flexibility. If the structure is too weak it won't provide support, but if it is too rigid it will just break. What you need is balance.

One of the new appointments at this client is from an HR background and has brought in organisational charts for the teams and re-mapped all the processes around these. All very effective, and a discipline that is necessary for sustaining the business, but we are already seeing a slowing in the ability to react to change because the decision is moving too far away from the point that it needs to be taken.

In this instance the structure has been designed around classic pyramids and my first problem is that they are drawn with the base at the bottom. From a psychological viewpoint I always like to see them drawn with the apex at the bottom to show that there is recognition that the leaders are there to support the organisation and not the other way round, but there is a bigger issue here in that the thinking is becoming dominated by these triangular family trees.

Fixed battle formations have their place and can be effective: The fighting square, as utilised by the Romans and others for example will wear down an opposing force, but if I am going to take a military theme what is needed in modern business is something far more flexible.

I'm reminded of the early days of aerial combat in WW2. The RAF had their fighter squadron battle formations and, on spotting the enemy the call would go out to assume attack formation three (or whatever). In the minute or so that this took to sort out the enemy were either a) somewhere else or b) shooting them down. The Luftwaffe had already worked out the formation of two pairs, each pair working as a leader and wingman. One of the beauties of this in a leadership context is that the pair can, and did, swap roles as their position relative to a target dictated, so that the leader would slip behind his number two and become the wingman for that attack.

So my point is that there are times within business teams that anyone can be the leader because that is what is needed at that moment. Most times this is through devolved authority so you don't have to ask a customer or colleague to wait while you consult your supervisor; you just do what you have to do to solve the problem. The organisation may be shaped by hierarchical diagrams, but the processes allow flexible reaction to whatever circumstances that have to be faced.

Leadership is about people; making sure that they know what is expected of them and trusting them to do their best for you. Yes we do need the organisational structure, but don't try to tie leadership to it. Allow the teams to work flexibly and to do what they need to when they need to do it. Here leadership has no fixed shape; it changes to suit the needs, and the leader one minute can be a follower the next if that is for the best.

Who is doing the leading and why does it matter?

Developing the theme of What Shape is Leadership, much of what being a good leader is about is in how they are perceived; the leader believes in themselves and their cause(s), others see this, relate to it and follow. Within the organisation this is fine as it is a relatively closed community, but business organisations exist to serve other communities, so how do these outsiders perceive leadership in your organisation?

My previous musings on who is doing the leading have been around there being many leaders in any group. Yes you have The Leader, but there are leaders of smaller groups amongst the followers and so on. In What Shape is Leadership I looked at how The Leader need not always be the leader depending on circumstances impacting on the organisation, and here I want to look at that from an external point of view.

If I am a customer (or supplier) I may well never see The Leader, and may never know who they are at all, but I do see leadership, or a lack of it, in my dealings with your business. So when we talk about customer service we are really talking about how that leadership is displayed in how the front line interacts with others.

When I talked about the shape of leadership last time I referred to the hierarchical pyramid that organisational charts depict, and my preference for drawing them upside down, but in a practical sense I see the shape as more of a fluid blob with the leader moving around in it. Richard Branson at Virgin may be one of the exceptions, but most of those outside of your blob, including those where the revenue comes from, only see the leader through the people at the edge that they touch.

I suggest that Leadership is not just about you and your interaction with your team or your business. In leading your people, there is an element of your leadership that you want them to reflect to all of those around them; to each other, as role models, and to those outside of your business, for example your customers and suppliers. Your leadership values are probably enshrined in your Corporate Social Responsibility (CSR) policy, but ought to be embedded in everything that your organisation is doing.

I once had what I called the Ghent Agenda (see Chapter 9), based on an experience in Belgium. We stopped off on our way home from Hanover only to find that the first hotel that we tried was full. The receptionist checked where I was headed for then rang her colleague at Ghent and booked us in there where further excellent service was received. My proposition is that when I deal with your business I will see leadership qualities displayed by your people in the way that we interact. If I am your customer I may not always be right, but how am I treated? If I am a supplier how do they react to me? If your people are well led the example should show through and, at that point in time, the face of the leader will be reflected in the person that I'm dealing with.

Equipping and empowering your people so that they can meet, or exceed, the standards you set has extraordinary power to generate success, but it also makes your leadership mean something tangible.

Back to the Floor Part One

I am a big fan of this. Those that haven't tried yet are, I think, missing out, especially in terms of their leadership qualities.

One of the key attributes, as we've discussed here and in the Leader's Cafe Foundation group on LinkedIn, is trust. As a leader, people need to believe in you to follow you, and one way of helping to build that trust is to let your team see you get in the trenches with them. You aren't competing with them to show that you can do their job better, or even as well, just to show them that you are willing to come and see the world from their viewpoint.

You have to take it seriously though; this isn't just a PR stunt, you have to get in there and do it. See what it is like to try and deliver the things you need to have done to achieve the goals that you have set. Ask about the problems and how they can be overcome. Ask what your front line would do to make it better. Offer your own suggestions and see how they feel about them. See how your customers react to the service that you are providing and ask them how they feel. Be prepared to defend things that have to be that way and explain why, but allow the challenge and look to see if there is another way.

The possibilities are endless and the potential value to you, your team and the business is enormous. I would urge you to try it. If you're wavering, just try a couple of hours, but I would suggest that you aim for a full day working the normal hours for the job you've selected. Switch off the mobile (cell) phone, forget your emails and focus on your new job.

What have I done lately? Well, in the last 18 months or so I have: driven a van delivering office supplies, worked in a customer service call centre, worked in the transport office booking deliveries, served as a line buyer working on basic consumable buying and on buying from the far east, driven a truck delivering furniture, provided the muscle for an office relocation and spent a night shift with security guards.

All of the clients that I have provided consultancy, mentoring and training services for have benefited in some way from these activities, usually because it has helped me spot the problems and work out solutions for them. It has helped the implementation of the solutions because the people who have been affected by the changes have bought into them knowing where the ideas have come from.

I pride myself in being someone that makes things happen. I run successful workshops for senior teams on how to implement strategy successfully, to execute as my US friends put it. One of the reasons I know how to make things happen is that I understand how the front line works and going there on a regular basis keeps my knowledge current.

No, it may not work for everyone. You need to have a thick skin and to be able to take the flack: Some front line teams would relish the thought that one of the "suits" was coming amongst them and will lay all sorts of things in your path. But if you can take that and prove yourself, then I promise you that you, and those that you've worked amongst, will have made a quantum leap in the right direction.

Back to the Floor Part Two

With just a little writing to do over the holidays, boredom was setting in, so, prompted by my own blog, a plot emerged to do a bit more back on the floor.

One of my core disciplines is logistics, and it is one of the more in demand areas for resource at the moment. We may be in recession, but stuff still needs shifting, so I got on to the one of my agency resource pals and registered as a driver, not for full-time work, but happy to take on the odd day at short notice.

One evening after dinner the phone rings; can I be at xxx RDC (Regional Distribution Centre) for 0345 tomorrow? Yes, and I was. Vehicle checked and running it is below freezing in the yard as I back onto bay 17 to load roll cages for a local run. Change of plan - take this load instead, another local run, this time out into Oxfordshire. Eight cages on and strapped and we're out of the yard heading east. The full, blue, moon is setting behind us and lighting the frozen fields. Rabbits are everywhere having breakfast and a badger races across the road, fortunately far enough ahead to make it safely as our 5 year old DAF trundles along. These things are, for me, the joy of driving. In all of those years wearing out the roads in my executive express it was what you could see on the way, differing seasons and time of day all bringing something to stir the spirit that kept me going.

Barely 30 minutes out of the RDC and we've arrived. The customer indicates where to tip (what a wonderful expression) so I park up and kill the engine.

We unload and I wait for the empty cages to take back. Last couple on to the tail lift and... the battery dies on me. Sure enough, can't turn the engine over and get Daisy DAF running, so there I am, blocking the yard, tail lift at half-mast and going nowhere.

I call the number in the cab for help and the fitter says he'll be 30 - 45 minutes, so I do what I can to keep warm and wait. I ring the transport office but they're not answering. A call to the main switchboard and someone says they'll pass on the message. Just over an hour later the rescue party arrives, jump starts me and I can close up and head back. Empties dropped I report back to the transport office to hear the lady in front of me telling them that truck 629 has broken down. That's me and I'm back I say. Too late for another run I'm offered the chance to fill out my 8 hour shift in the warehouse, so I spend the next 5 hours or so on my feet moving boxes. Not as much fun for me as driving, but we get some banter going and there is the camaraderie of common purpose so the time passes easily.

Home mid-day and starting to feel sore from using muscles I'd forgotten I had. An interesting day; I've had a glimpse from the inside of how that business functions, experienced its transport and seen how it coped with a problem, seen at first hand some of its processes and how it treats its own people and agency bods like me. And I've met and worked with some interesting people as well has having enjoyed my, albeit brief, nocturnal run in the country.

Two days later, 0716. I get a 'phone call from the agency night duty. Can I cover a sick absence driving a 5 ton drop side for a local building supplies company? No problem, I can be there in about 45 minutes and my to do list of phone calls and writing can wait a day.

I report in and check my vehicle, a 2 year old Mercedes. Checks completed we start to load a variety of timber and other items. I'm used to box vans and fairly cubic loads from my occasional forays into driving so this is all new to me and I have to seek help from the yard guys and watch a couple of customers loading and securing their own vehicles to pick up the methods used. Load secured I collect my instructions; the load is for a construction site in the town (new houses) and then I need to head north to pick up a pallet of roof tiles from a wholesaler.

I carry my own sat nav, but it is of limited use for a construction site as the address won't yet exist, so I have general directions and work it out from there. I strike lucky and arrive without problems. I get the run around a bit from the builders, but find the foreman and, having waited for a space on site to be cleared, reverse in to get the load off. It's bitter cold and the load is awkward, but they have a fork lift and we clear the truck. Paperwork signed I return to the cab to find that my offside front wheel is parked on a small piece of ground that isn't frozen solid and has sunk up to the axle! With the caterpillar tracked Bobcat pulling and 3 hefty builders pushing we manage to extricate the truck after about 20 minutes of concerted effort. I thank the lads and head off out of town to get my next load.

Here we have a very professional set up. A big yard with a lot of traffic variety and a very tight health & safety set up. My briefing on signing in is comprehensive and I join the queue for loading, but it is a slick operation and I'm on my way quickly back to the yard, stopping to fill up with diesel on the way.

Back at the yard I'm told that my roof tiles are to stay on and be delivered to a village school 20 odd miles away, and then I have a run down towards Trowbridge. I consult with the yard guys and we agree that if we put the tiles by the tailboard we can get the other load on around them and I can do one round trip instead of two. The office team don't seem impressed by use of initiative to save time and mileage and just shrug, so we load up. If there's a fork lift at the first drop we can take their tiles off over the tail, if not it's a handball job. Either way I can then head off across country to the second drop.

Off we go south and out into the country. The low sun is blinding, but I'm tall and have the seat raised so it's not too bad for me, and the frozen hills look magnificent bathed in light. The view from my cab is great. Deer roam in the fields and I'm enjoying getting to grips with handling the Mercedes. Getting to the first drop involves some single track roads and between the high banks in a couple of places the road is still sheet ice, so slow and steady is the way to go.

The school is in a tiny hamlet and parked cars need to be negotiated with not much room to spare. I can reverse into the site without trouble, but getting out will be interesting. No fork lift so we handball off the pallet of tiles. Getting a signature takes a moment as they are off up their ladders like a shot. The resultant scribble I could probably enter for the Turner prize, but it will have to do. No-one to help me with the couple of shunts to get out of the yard and head back the way I came, so I get out and assess each shunt, but I'm soon rolling again and enjoy about an hour of villages, hills and wildlife as I head west across the county.

Once again, this is why I love driving and time passes quickly. All too soon I'm at the village for my drop, another new housing development. Unloading is easy with the aid of a big fork truck and I'm off to find a lay-by for a late lunch and my statutory break. Back at the yard there's nothing more so I'm off home after a great 7 hour shift.

With both jobs I've had an insight into new things; I've never had a (truck) breakdown before, I've learned about loading and securing odd shaped stuff onto a drop side so that getting it off in a tight space can be safe and easy. I've seen some very skilled people at work first hand and seen good and bad examples of management and process. I'm physically fitter than I was the week before and that's got to be a good thing and my grey cells have been challenged by the new working environments and the challenges they presented to me. I've brought both vehicles back undamaged and completed all of my deliveries and collections as required. I've learned from others and been able to add my own contribution. All of these things I will take forward to working with future clients and my contribution will be enhanced because of it.

I've also seen first-hand what might be a couple of green shoots of recovery: If the housing market is a key indicator then seeing two housing developments recommencing work on building has to be a positive sign? I hope so.

But there are another couple of benefits, very personal ones for me. The first is the satisfaction of having done an honest day's toil. I find that there is something very comforting about having laboured and exercised the body, even if I am sore in places as a result.

The second is from what I have seen on my drives. The higher cab of a truck enables a different view than from my car, and both the night and day rides through the rolling countryside around where I live, the wildlife, farm animals, villages, hills and valleys, all in their winter finery, truly lifted my spirits. The second run of the second job in particular was a magical afternoon and I would not have experienced it had I not had this train of thought for last week's blog. So thanks to those of you who follow these musings and prompt my thoughts; it led to me having a really great experience.

Try getting back to the floor and, if you do, do it properly. You'll find it very worthwhile.

Chapter Three - People Power

Leadership does not exist without followers, so your people are vital. Real leaders know and understand this.

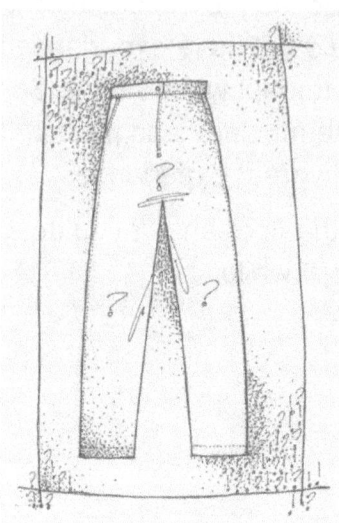

I Don't Have My Decision Making Trousers On!

It came at the end of a long day. The Wokingham Wonder and I had got home from our respective offices, fed the cats and were into that round of what shall we eat, watch on TV, and do at the weekend routine that you go through. I'd been making decisions all day, but tired, and changed into golf shirt and slacks, my ability to make a decision seemed to have vanished into the wardrobe along with the power suit. "I don't have my decision making trousers on" I said in a moment of bemused spontaneity: The expression entered legend at home and at work.

The art of decision making is being able to make the important ones; to weigh up what you know, and then to decide on a course of action. The elements that are missing there though are time, resource and risk. These need to be balanced and this where the art of decision making comes in. How much time do you have? How much resource do you have? What are the risks?

Time may or may not be of the essence. If your initial consideration is that you don't know enough to make an informed decision, you might decide to defer until you can find out more about your options or about the consequences. If you do have time, then fine, use it well, but if you haven't then you have to go with what you do know.

What resources do you need deploy to implement your decision? If you are well informed, then you will know how much you have, if not you are flying blind. As we have just discussed, you may not have time to find out, so an important factor in decision making is having your finger on the pulse.

And then we come to the risks. One of the early lessons I learned as a manager was that you either did something or you didn't. In either case other things were going to happen regardless, so the first element in making a decision is what if I do nothing? You can then weigh up the implications of that against any course(s) of action that you are contemplating and make your decision accordingly. Every decision has an element of risk attached.

As leaders we are expected to make decisions (especially the hard ones) and our people rightly judge us on the quality of them as do our peers and our superiors. Some of my loneliest moments have been the times when the hard decisions have had to be made, but that's what pays the big bucks. By all means take advice and seek guidance, but in the end you have to take responsibility.

With a big decision I try to document my thinking, both to aid the decision making and for posterity. It sometimes can be useful to do a balance sheet of factors for and against to help clarify the issues, and having that to look back on and review your thinking when you have the benefit of knowing the outcome. I think that that approach has helped me get better at making decisions, but has also helped me explain to my team how and why I got to the answer that I did.

But it isn't just the big boss that has to make decisions, and they can't make them all in any case; the team has to be able to make their own calls along the way, so developing their skills is fundamental.

One of the things I have done at times with my teams to help them make their own decisions is to tell them that, like the genie, I only have three decisions available for them that day. I'll support them in making their own, and allow them to get them wrong from time to time because they won't learn otherwise; you have to learn the art by doing.

Develop Your People and Thrive!

I had just taken part in a discussion on the problem of having key team members headhunted. Others were complaining about the loss of key team members and talking about refusing to let people go on internal promotions, or at least delaying their departure.

I have no qualms about headhunting as an employer. If I lose members of my team this way it means that my people are seen as high calibre. Word gets round on these things and you get a reputation as a place that people can get a career boost from, so you attract better quality people.

Why would you want to stand in someone's way in any case? You may want to keep them to deliver a result that makes you look good, but is their heart going to be in it if they know that you are blocking their progression? You could be running the risk of turning a good team player into a resentful rotten apple and how are other people on your team going to view it? They'll see the same thing potentially going to happen to them down the line.

If you have a succession plan in place you'll be bringing other good people through to fill the gaps, so let people go with a smile.

Success breeds success. Invest in people, enjoy the benefits of having them with you while they are there, and wish them well when they go.

If the Boss Doesn't Come to Work, Who'll Notice?

In one of my Monday Musing blogs I asked Who Is The Most Important Person In Your Company? The answer was that they all were, because everyone is contributing something, otherwise why are you employing them?

There was a time when I went through a phase of thinking that, as a junior manager, but in a high profile role, I was the big cheese; it was all about me. I had the ideas, I made the plans, and I delivered the results. To a degree my superiors and their peers encouraged this by heaping praise on me as I rolled over objective after objective, but I could easily have ensured that the plaudits were shared. I didn't.

Then came a moment when I was addressing a group about what we had achieved and, as sometimes happens when I am in that sort of position, I had one of those moments where my mouth was on autopilot delivering the well-rehearsed messages, part of my brain was outside looking in and it occurred to me what a pompous pratt I was. "Just listen to this c**p" as voice was saying in my ear, and that voice was right. It dawned on me that here I was taking the credit for something that might have had a lot of me in it, but would not have happened if not for the efforts of others. I might have been the quarterback calling the plays and distributing the ball to make those plays, but there were the others on the field, the backroom people and all sorts of other unsung heroes without whose contributions I would have gone from hero to zero myself in short order.

It might have taken a while to get that message home to me, but once it had slammed home I didn't forget and I've carried it with me ever since.

Fast forward about 7 years. By this time I have been a senior manager for some time, but with the knowledge that the results that got me there were all team efforts. My boss squared has dug us into a bit of a hole and the troops are not happy.

I have called a mass meeting in an attempt to head off the trade union seeking a mandate to include industrial action. I'm on the back foot and having to work to timetables that others are creating. Upwards of 350 people are gathered in the warehouse and a small stack of pallets has been placed for me to stand on and face them.

My team are nervous and so am I, but I'm trying to show confidence which is a little difficult as I don't have a clue what I am going to say. I know what I need to communicate, but how to do it?

Half an hour later my team and I have left the scene to let the union officials have their say. How has it gone? Shortly afterwards we hear that the audience has dispersed and we are told that the union have not got their mandate for action. There is a slight sense of relief, but we know we have work to do to bring back a decent working relationship.

So what did I say to help bring this about? Well there was no transcript or recording, but the gist of it was to try and explain that they were the key to making a success of what we were doing, and the crux of my argument was that if I was missing for an hour they wouldn't notice, if I was missing for a week they still wouldn't notice. If I was missing for a month they'd notice that the overtime hadn't been authorised, but not much else. Yet if they were missing for an hour the place would stop and nothing would happen. If we didn't do anything for a day let alone a week then we would have no income and would close. We would all be out of jobs.

So they needed to recognise their importance as much as I did, but they also needed to accept that they had the same responsibility to each other as I did to them. I would work my socks off to make sure that we had clients, that we had the equipment and everything else that was needed to do the job, but it was them that did the job. If they chose to not do it then that was their decision, but it had consequences for all of us and that included them.

It was all off the cuff, but from the heart and it was true. This was not a load of management speak, it was plain talking, and it came from the lessons that I learned the hard way that it is the team that succeeds, not the leader.

The essential truth of my message was that if I didn't go into work for a day, it would make no difference. If any one of us didn't for in for a day it would make no difference, but if I went in and they all took the day off we would have a problem. It is the team as a whole that delivers to results, not any individual working alone.

So look after your people, without them you are nothing.

Staff; a Quick Rant.

This is a personal crusade to end the practice of referring to employees as "The/My Staff". The staff is the big pole outside that you run the flag up on special days. The people working for the organisation are just that; the people.

As a leader, when you have to refer to these people, use "My (Our) People", or "My (Our) Team, or, better still, "My Colleagues".

So, unless you have your own personal flagpole, no more references to The or My Staff please.

Thank You.

Recognition

Recognition is often paired with Reward in terms of motivation, and to most people that means do a good job and you'll get a treat, but I want to explore here a much wider view of what Recognition should mean to a leader.

Yes, Recognition is about recognising performance, but not just the good. You have to recognize the bad and the ugly as well. You can shower rewards around as much as you like, but if you don't confront all levels of performance your people will see through you. Celebrate success by all means, but be equally frank when there has been a screw up and talk as openly about that.

This is not about apportioning blame; it is about looking at poor performance and how to put things right. Criticize the performance, not the person; there is a subtle difference. Working with teams or individuals on making them better is as much of a motivator as rewarding them for a job well done.

As a leader you should be ensuring that the area you are responsible for is pulling its weight. You'll be implementing the business strategy and deploying the necessary tactics to achieve goals. You need to be on top of people's performance and be able to recognise where there may be issues and find out what they are. The sooner you can address a problem the quicker you can fix it, and if you can fix it before it gets out of hand then you give everyone a shot at any performance based rewards that may be on offer.

This isn't micro managing though, you have to trust people and ensure that they are aware of that trust, but your people are trusting you to be watching their backs, so if there is someone who looks like drowning they will be looking to you for help.

There is a strong team building element here where you can build individual and group goals that encourage mutual support within the group. So have a plan and make sure everyone knows it and their part in it. Monitor progress towards key milestones, not just through numbers or reports, but by looking and asking the right questions of people and spot potential problems early and fix them.

Another area that gets overlooked is that people see recognition as something that flows down the chain of command. Traditionally that's true, but what about recognition in other directions? For a start there are your peers. If one of them, or their team/division has done well why not say so? You do see this from time to time, quite often in my experience it's Sales thanking Operations for actually managing to deliver what it was that they'd sold the client, or Operations thanking Sales for selling something that they can deliver (hey, I'm sort of kidding here), but a quiet word or patting a colleague on the back can be worth a huge amount to the recipient. When did you last say "well done" to the person next to you in the conference room when they sat down after making a presentation?

Stepping it up a gear, have you ever said "good job" to your boss? Have you ever emailed the CEO to say that you read their interview in the paper/magazine and felt that they had done you all proud as a business?

OK, so maybe some will see that as brown nosing, but it doesn't have to be. Now if you really want to get serious about this principle, how about saying "I think you got that wrong" to someone further up the line? Recognition is about performance - at all levels.

The Importance of Good People

Doesn't it just lift you when you get to work with good people?

By the middle of 2009 I had been working as an independent consultant for over a year. Not only was the global recession making it harder to win new clients and work, get a commitment from those that did want you to start a project and to get those that you had worked for to pay you, but I had also had a couple of spells where I was out of action to have and recuperate from operations.

With the second operation behind me I was into the hard grind of finding some work and very much in need of a boost. Let no-one kid you that business success comes easy.

As I started the second week in June that year I had two meetings in my diary, one with a new contact and one with a guy that I've not seen for 7 or 8 years. Both meetings turned out to be really positive, swapping ideas and sparking off each other.

With all of these sort of meetings I'm looking for mutual benefit, not just for my contacts and I, but for the people in their organisations, their customers and suppliers and so on.

OK, so there's a recession, but we'll come out of it, and meeting positive people, good people enhances my confidence.

So have a think about who you know within a reasonable travelling distance. Look through your LinkedIn, Facebook or Twitter contacts, old colleagues or whatever and try and invite a couple of people for coffee or lunch. You just never know where it will lead and, in any case, time spent with good people is time well spent.

How Do You Know That You Are a Leader?

I've always found that running a training course or seminar tends to teach me something. I know that the point is that I am supposed to be imparting knowledge to those that have come to listen and have often paid for their place, but the learning is two way.

The first phase is when I work through my material because that gets me thinking about what I will say, how to say it, how to adjust things for a specific audience and so on. The process of considering and refining is a learning opportunity as I check and research aspects of the material I will use, the anecdotes that I will tell and any incidents that I will refer to.

But the greatest opportunity to learn is in the discussion around the group when the material is delivered. The questions that are raised, especially the ever powerful "Why?" are a great opportunity to learn. Having your thinking challenged may not always be comfortable, but it is a great way for the whole group to learn, myself included.
There is an old adage, out of the mouths of babes and innocents, and it is very true that the less knowledge your audience has of your subject the greater the challenge of explaining it simply and clearly.
Again, the opportunity for you to learn in these circumstances is huge. It isn't that you don't know the answer as much as being able to recall the information, phrase it in your head and deliver it effectively without appearing to be ruffled. The ability to improvise on a theme is a skill that you learn by practice.

This week I was asked a wonderful question when talking to a group of mid-teenagers about leadership. "When did you first know you were a leader?" Before I could answer another came in with the equally wonderful "How do you know you are a leader?"

I've been asked variations of these questions before many times, but always when working with individuals or small groups of people who are at the early stage of their management career. I use management here rather than leadership because, whilst there needs to be an overlap, most organisations promote or recruit on management skills and expect leadership rather than the other way round.

But how to answer a group of people aged around 15 or 16? So I told them that one of the things that you find out about learning is that you often don't know that you know something until you have to use it, or the opposite in that you think you know how to do something, but find that when you try it out, you don't. And I told them a story about one of my early attempts at leadership.

I was 19 years old and had had some experience of being in charge, of being responsible, but I was given a job that meant I had to supervise 4 part time clerks. They were all ladies and two worked mornings and the other two worked afternoons. They all knew their jobs better than I did and the team worked well enough. Or at least they did until I arrived.

What I should have done was to keep a light hand on the tiller and let them get on with the work, but instead I interfered; micro managed them as we might call it in today's management speak. The result was that they did what I told them and not what they needed to do to keep things flowing. My world began to fall apart on day two and I had to be pulled out of the fire before the week was out.

Sure, they were as in the wrong as I was, but that isn't the point. I learned the hard way that a new broom can sweep too clean and, as my boss pointed out, the team's leader needs to know what the objective is, to communicate that effectively and then to allow the team to use their experience to deliver it.

It's one thing to know what your team do, but you can't do it all yourself, that's why you have employees. Make sure that they are trained, that they know what the process is and what the goals are, then let them get on with delivering. They will thrive on your trust and, when you are in that position with your team, you'll know that you are leading.

Good leaders know that it's all about the people really.

Chapter Four - Talking Teams

Whether you want to talk about teams or tribes or any other way of describing your followers, they will become a family to you, and you need to devote the same sort of energies on nurturing them that you do on your family.

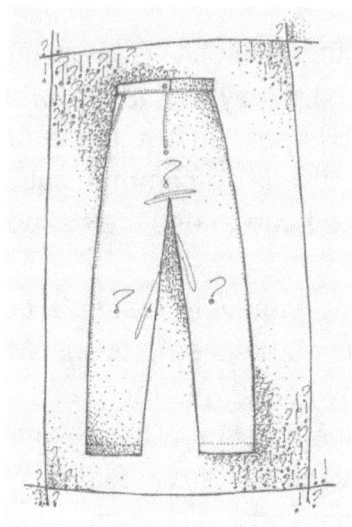

Feedback

For me, and no doubt for many others of my generation, feedback was what you got when your guitar got too close to your amp. Some could make it musical; Beck, Page, Clapton, Hendrix et al, but for most of us it was just a horrible screeching noise that we could do little with and added nothing to the song that we were (trying to) play.

For those of us in work, your guvnor would have a quiet word, or a loud shout, now and again and your workmates would straighten you out when necessary (many is the peg I've been taken down).

Then suddenly feedback was a management buzz word. Having a quiet word was really feedback, and it was ever so valuable (a loud shout was also feedback, but this was frowned upon, more so when they started to call it harassment).

I've been in a little discussion thread on feedback recently on LinkedIn, and the instigator made a very valid point about the recipient. I completely agree with that. People are different and you should treat them accordingly. Good leaders know how to give good feedback, bad leaders don't, and it doesn't matter how many standard ways of doing it that are cascaded down it won't make a bad leader a good one or turn poor feedback into something that can be used to improve. Feedback of the wrong sort will be on a par with the screeching noise I started this item on.

Call it what you like, but me? I'm going to carry on talking to people about their performance in the way I've learned to do it, taking what works from the good people I've worked for, and avoiding the stuff the bad ones have inflicted. And when I come across people practicing the latter, I'll talk to them about why I think that they are doing it wrong.

And when someone comes to me and tells me I'm wrong, I'll listen, just like I always have, and try to improve myself accordingly. That approach has stood me in good stead as I've built many good teams; not fancy management speak, just being prepared to speak openly and fairly to people about how they are doing.

I don't agree with you, but that doesn't mean I don't like you

Reading the Sunday papers today I remarked on an interview with an eminent politician of years gone by. "But you hate him" was the response from the Berkshire Belle down the other end of the sofa.

We no, I don't hate them. I just don't agree with virtually everything that this person stands for. But that is the whole point for me: This is someone who has stuck to their views for as long as I can remember (and I think that they became an MP in the year that I was born), but they have never let their disagreement with others become personal as far as I can tell and, whilst I fundamentally disagree with their politics I have a huge respect for them.

And that is the difference. Over the years that I have played the game of corporate snakes & ladders I've tried to adopt the principle of critique the idea not the person. I have worked for and with people that I have got on with well on a personal level, but have had a nightmare professional relationship, and others with whom I have got on well with in the business sense, but have had no desire whatsoever to have any social contact with.

It isn't a black and white issue for me; there is a whole spectrum of colour to relationships, and this is one of the keystones of leadership. You can't please all of the people all of the time and you can't like them either, and nor can they all like you. What you have to be able to do is to recognise and draw out the things in others that the team needs.

In fact the statement that "I don't like you, but that doesn't mean that I don't agree with you" is equally true.

Having people around me that don't always agree with me is crucial in my teams. I want to have that level of healthy friction to drive the team forward.

So in my teams I have always striven to earn the respect of others, and to offer my respect to them and their abilities. Have we all liked each other? Often, but not always, and I believe that that is one of the reasons why so many of my teams have been so good. I talked earlier about the benefits of friction within a team or other business relationship if it is well managed and this is another good example of applying that principle.

The last thing that I want is a team of yes people. I want those who will be prepared to challenge me when they genuinely believe that I am wrong, and I welcome those who want my job. Yes, even that, because when there is the opportunity of something better for me I can honestly point out that I have one or more worthy successors on my team alone.

Thoughts on Simplicity and Trust

My thoughts here are around a couple of basic points at the heart of leadership. They started in looking at the perversity of the simplest actions often being the hardest to do well and into this mix came the issue of trust. This line of thought had been prompted by some work I was doing with a client to help the new management team bed in some new members and start to make things happen to deliver more of the growth that their business has enjoyed over the last year.

I have been a senior manager since the mid 1980s and have experienced all of the "latest big thing" trends that have come and gone over that period. There was (is) nothing wrong with any of them, and if they didn't work for people it was almost certainly because they weren't properly implemented (and I saw plenty of that). No, they are mostly fine for one simple reason; they are all based on simple principles. Good honest common sense in fact.

That some consultancies made millions out of them is because simple things are often hard to do and people need help along the way. No matter how complex a problem is though, it is only a series of simple steps. As a former computer programmer I have experienced breaking tasks down into a simple sequence of instructions and decisions to enable the computer to perform them in fractions of a second and make it look easy and the process is the same for anything complicated or difficult. There are various sayings around this; eating the elephant one bite at a time or a journey of a thousand miles starts with a single step being just two that come to mind.

It is the same for a business. The business world can be very complex, but there are some basic truths that are at the heart of it all. You are in business to make a profit. Profit means earning more than you spend and you need to keep the cash coming through the door faster than you spend it. If you are selling something you have to know what it is so that you can explain it to your customers. You have to tell people that you are selling it or they won't know that they can buy it from you. I could go on, but these are all very simple things that can get very complicated, and when that happens people don't always do them well and, sometimes, don't do them at all.

As a sole trader you have responsibility for it all, but when you start to grow, you have to take on people to help. Your business structure become more complex and doing simple things can become more difficult if you allow it to. The key to being able to keep doing the difficult stuff is to be able to do the easy things well and to keep doing them well. This is where trust enters the equation.

Trust in this context is about being able to show weakness without fear of ridicule or sanction. It is about trusting colleagues to be signed up to the common goal of success rather than personal glory. I use sports as a regular example because it shows the trait in both lights. Good sports teams work for the common good, but how often do you see a potentially good side perform poorly because one or two members are more interested in their own results?

In business a team who trust each other and do simple things well will always succeed.

You Can't Take Yourself Too Seriously

"You can't take yourself too seriously. If you do you are buying your own con." Ferrol Sams

It's a quote I found in a book entitled Last Bus to Albuquerque and it struck a chord with me when I first read it back in 1994. I used the first half of it as one of my over the desk mottos; the whole thing was too long and, in any case, if anyone thought that I was a con artist I didn't want anything over my desk that appeared to confirm that view!

But the sentiment is a strong one, and it took a while for me to realise that I had fallen into the trap of taking myself very seriously indeed; the blinding flash that showed me what a complete idiot I was making of myself was an unpleasant moment. As I write these words now I am transported back to about 1984 when I had that moment on the road to Damascus so to speak.

Having been able to see the problem and deal with it made a big difference to me in many ways, both professional and personal. I began to enjoy myself and I got even better at what I did as a result. When I adopted the strap line of "25 years of having fun whilst making things happen" last year that is exactly what I meant.

Getting a laugh out of every day isn't always easy, and there have been times when black humour has won through. I won't repeat some of the jokes here because I recognise that they were offensive to some, but in the context of our team and the moment they were just what we needed to lift the mood. The best ones were, of course, the ones that punctured my dignity and I'll share a couple here.

My team and I managed a diverse property estate and most of the team would have to travel to get to a common location, so hotels provided a neutral venue, but at the previous couple of meetings I had felt it necessary to mention standards of dress; we were on show and the welcome board in reception told everyone which company we represented. After the second warning one of the team challenged me quietly and suggested that suits and ties were maybe too formal, so could we not have a smart casual regime, maybe golf clubhouse standards? I took the point and smart casual was the order of the day for the next meeting. I turned up in golf shirt and chinos to find the rest all in their best business suits - game set and match to the team.

Another time I had been banging the environmental drum and we had begun to have our site vehicles and equipment painted green in an effort to raise awareness amongst our tenants and generally push the Green boat out. Then came a meeting to discuss the issue of the latest set of site manuals for our tenants. "I suppose you want green binders?" I was asked, and the answer was, of course, "Yes". On leaving that meeting I was reminded that I should wear overalls when on that site as it was both protocol and would be part of the new Health & Safety plan in respect of wearing personal protective equipment (lead from the front John). I mentioned, sheepishly, that my girth had outgrown my overalls and that a new set were needed. No problem, they'd be waiting for me on my next visit. And they were, in lurid green! Team 10, Bowen 0.

You can't take yourself too seriously.

You Have What You've Got, Use It Well and More Will Come

This wasn't written with the financial crisis in mind, but, in proof reading it, it could well have been. My thoughts were more on developing teams and, because teams are made up of them, individuals.

If you lived in that ideal world of fluffy bunnies and blue skies then you could always pick your own team. Fortunately, at least for me, we don't live there. It wouldn't be much fun anyway as there would be no challenges, and so back here in the real world we will, as leaders, have to make something of what we have.

Starting with ourselves, we start with whatever latent talent we are born with and what our parents give us. Then teachers, peer groups, the media and others add to the mix and off we go to work. We're constantly adding to what we started with and do have choices about what we take on and what we discard. We absorb knowledge, hone that with practice to gain experience and, perhaps, wisdom. How we use what we have is our choice; to do well is a choice and so is mediocrity. Doing well doesn't mean getting to the top; there is that Martin Luther King quote about the street sweeper and, if that is your calling, doing it well to the best of your abilities.

When you get you first team it will be one that you inherit. It may well not even have been put together by your predecessor and just be the result of the way the company you work for operates its promotions. So what can you do? Well first, let everyone know what the goals are. At this stage they're going to be handed down to you, but let everyone know that you're signed up and committed. Then get to know your team, get to find out what makes them tick. Do the same with their people. Making personal contact is vital (at one time I could have named every one of my 350 strong workforce and I still can name most of them if I meet them in the street 20 years after moving on).

Help the team play to their strengths. Where someone is weak in one area you need to both coach them and get the rest of the team helping back them. It isn't hard to get a team to the point where they will fight for each other. And don't worry about having a mix in your team - would a soccer team buy the 11 best goalkeepers and send them out on Saturday? Would you field 15 running backs in the NFL? Top teams are made up of a mixture of skills and attitudes.

As time goes on you will lose someone. Probably the first to go will be the best because they will gain a promotion, but don't worry about that. If fact the more often it happens the better, because you will get a reputation for running a team that people can progress from and the better people will want to come and work for you.

You will, of course, at some time have to deal with underperformance. There will be someone who, despite your best efforts at coaching and support, and in providing training, will just not make the grade. You have to deal with this using the process available within your company, and do it in a fair and timely manner. Ducking the issue just makes it worse for everyone, so do it right and do it when you have to.

Working well with what you have will develop you, your people and the business you work for. Your career will move forward as will the careers of those that you help. You have what you've got: Use it well and more will come.

Teams Are Made Up of Individuals

A team is a collection of individuals, but if you get the mix right and develop them then the sum of their efforts will be greater than the sum of the individual contributions. They call this synergy. In the previous though I talked about sports teams and proposed that you would not field a team made up of the same specialisms. But what about a team made up of the finest individuals in each position? Well, I would suggest that that might not work too well either, because such teams often contain too many people who are more concerned about their own reputations than that of the team. We've all witnessed some high profile failures of that nature.
It is slightly academic though, because in business life we often have to use what we have, but that is not a barrier to success. The key is to start by identifying people's strengths and getting everyone playing to those. Don't worry about weaknesses to start with, or at least don't let on that you are concerned about them. The key to positive results is positive people, so you want to accentuate anything good.

Positive results then help to breed more positive people; you get that upward spiral. As these results come through and the confidence of the team rises then you can start to work on any areas of weakness. How you do this depends on the person and the issue; some will take it on the chin, some will come to you and ask for help, others will need more subtle handling, but it can be good to let people share their weaknesses with the team. Vulnerability is a powerful tool in building trust and the sort of mutual support that great teams demonstrate.

One of my most successful teams was quite short lived; less than a year after we had formed half of them had been promoted into better roles and a corporate re-shuffle finished us off, but this team was made up of people who had all been rejected from other roles in an earlier re-organisation and several of them had been deemed not good enough to retain the role that they had been in.

I was also dumped on this crew as, at the eleventh hour, a personnel issue required a change in the allocation of senior management roles and I was asked to step down from the one I had been appointed to and swap with a colleague. I wasn't happy, but saw the problem and walked away from a cracking role that I really wanted to take what everyone regarded as the corporate equivalent of a posting to Antarctica.

The next day I met with my new team. I knew them all by sight, and a couple a little better. Morale was on the floor and we were in trouble, so I took a very high risk strategy and went for the underdog play. They knew that I had been inked in for another job and so I opened with the line "Welcome to the first meeting of the rejects club". I told them that we had a job, a pay packet and something to prove.

We turned that team around and made a spectacular difference, but it was a close run thing. The underdog mentality had to be teased out of the equation once we started to get the results, but it was hard work to change one or two people away from it and, whilst they did re-build their careers, they didn't pick up promotions as others did. That doesn't mean that they were failures though; as I said at the start, teams are individuals, and that means that they have their individual needs, ambitions and skill levels.

There are not as many CEO jobs as there are in middle management. There is no shame in being a good middle manager; we need a lot of them.

Teams are made up of people, and any group of people can be made into a good team if you play to their strengths.
So What About The Wider Team?

I've tended to refer to teams here as your peers or your direct reports, but all of the folks you have working for you are your team as well. They are also individuals and you need a balanced mix here too. If someone wants to come in, do their 8 hours or whatever to the best of their ability then go home and forget it then I'm OK with that; I need people like that.
But I also want people who are going to stretch themselves, who want to improve and to get on. I need some who want my job bad enough to come after it.
Within the mix of people that you have in your team it doesn't matter what they do for you during the working day, as long as they do their best, as much as their other interests and ambitions. Within a group of, say, 100 workers you will find an astonishing array of skills and talents most of which play no real part in that person's day job, but could if you let it and they are happy to let you.

Let's look at that group of 100. Regardless of sex you will find probably at least 30% run some sort of outside group; a sports team or league or some sort of club. Another 20% or so may well have a second job that deploys a different skill set. 20% or so will be earning extra income through party plan or catalogue selling and maybe 15% will have some sort of musical or artistic skill that they take outside of the home in some way.

To give some examples from just one of my teams, this one 350 strong: I had three people who sold their art work commercially, over 40 ran sports teams or leagues and more than 20 sang or played music on a semi pro basis. One was one of only eight people in the UK to have a licence to breed a specific type of monkey outside of zoological bodies and I had so many people almost doubling their income from direct sales schemes that I never got to count them all. And then there were a dozen or so who ran mobile DJ businesses and one was a regular on hospital radio as a volunteer, and voluntary work opens up a new vista of skills.

So you may view your workforce as a group of office or manufacturing or retail or whatever people, but you have this undercurrent of talent that is there to be tapped if you, and they, are willing to let it happen.

Within the wider team you have this wide range of abilities. Get to know your people, their interests and what makes them tick. If anyone resists let them, respect their privacy and move on, because there will be some who are happy to let you in. Even if those people don't want to let you help them develop latent skills into advancing their career, the fact that you have taken an interest in them will bring them into your fan club, and, as a leader, you need to have as many of your wider team in your fan club as you can get..

Setting The Tone

Something very important for the leader to do is to maintain a steady personal state; don't get too excited about success and don't get gloomy over failure. When times are hard you need to keep that positive feeling going, so keep up a steady stream of encouragement to your people. That's not to say provide false optimism, because that will not fool anyone, but the team will have a hard time keeping their heads up and battling on if they see that the leader is giving up.

This is all about trust and confidence again, two vital tools for the leader to learn how to use.

Chapter Five - Meaningful Meetings

It is a fact that we will all spend a large part of our working lives in meetings, so anything that helps make that time productive and enjoyable is worth doing.

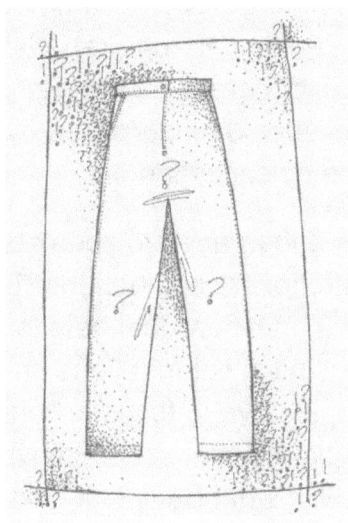

Making Meetings Matter

All too often meetings are a waste of time for all present, and therefore for the organisation that they represent. I'm often brought in to help teams on this problem and I regularly come across teams who don't even know whether they have decided anything at their meetings, let alone what it was. So how can you make meetings better?

First rule - all mobile phones switched off and put on a side table out of reach - no exceptions! Lap tops also turned off and put away. Meetings are about the people, so focus on each other and work together without outside distractions.

The meeting should be about the future, with everyone present informing the group about what they need to do and by when to hit (or exceed) their numbers, with the chair ensuring that each point is properly summed up and a clear action understood. People can read reports on progress before the meeting and there is no point in doing these to death again. No-one should be surprised by the numbers, so comments should be by exception only.

Everyone should be encouraged to speak on each point, but there has to be control over contributions. There has to be a limit to how often any one individual gets to speak on any one item, and I often limit initial contributions on any point to 3 minutes so that people have to focus on what they need to get over, and let them come back in once, maybe twice in debate. If someone agrees with what Betty just said then they can say so, but don't let them go over the same point again.

Once an item has gone round the table twice, the chair should sum up and seek agreement. Make sure that everyone understands what has been agreed, who is doing it and by when. Get the team signed up for the majority view regardless of which way they voted, and move on as a team, accepting collective responsibility for the decision.

Agendas need to be realistic. There is no point in allowing an hour for something that can be dealt with in 30 minutes, nor should something that needs 90 minutes be given a 20 minute slot. Think about the agenda and run it to time. Meetings that finish much earlier than planned are a criminal waste. Yes, everyone can find something to do with the time, but they could have found something much better to do with it if they knew about it in advance and could plan.

Use PowerPoint sparingly. It's great when used properly to inform people, but it can stifle discussion, and meetings should be about people interacting.

Don't interrupt or talk across people or hold side discussions while someone else is talking, and only critique ideas, never the individual expressing them; nothing should ever be allowed to become personal. A good chair should sort this out, but everyone should be accountable for their own actions.

With action points, make sure that they are confirmed as the meeting winds up. Try to make sure that everyone has an action, even if it is in support of someone else. If nothing has come out of the meeting for someone, then they can be tasked with bringing an issue to the next meeting to present on. Don't make it artificial, but do try to make sure that people are involved in contributing.

For Any Other Business try to limit people to no more than 1 item each. If it was that important they should have got it onto the main agenda, and no important topics should be hidden away in AOB.

Why Meet At All?

Have you ever been to a meeting where you quickly find that you are all in agreement and you're done and dusted in half an hour? I have, more than once, although it is the exception rather than the rule.

When information has been circulated to people and various sub sets of the people who would attend the proposed meeting have discussed the matter in hand it may well be that you don't really need to meet. Instead you could just email round to everyone and ask them if they are happy to sign up to the proposed outcome.

One of the biggest wastes is the routine meeting that just happens because of routine. Nothing much actually gets done, maybe a little sharing of progress or activity since the last meeting, all of which could have been circulated in reports for people to read (often it is, but folks will meet anyway). Meetings only really become relevant when there is something that is best resolved by round the table debate to allow a reasoned outcome to be decided and to have resources and timetables attached to it.

So be sure that you really need a meeting before you call one, and if you are stuck in a rut of meetings that just get held because you've always held them, then challenge that need. You could be freeing up a lot of productive time.

Mobile Phones, Laptops (and other similar devices) at Meetings

I've mentioned it earlier, but if you are at a meeting you are there for a reason and leaving your mobile (cell) phone on is both rude and unprofessional.

It's rude because you should be respecting your colleagues and devoting your full attention to the meeting.

It's unprofessional because your job for the duration of the meeting is to participate in what is being discussed and decided.

Distractions like phones should play no part. Turn them off and put them away out of sight. No leaving them on the desk in silent mode; switch off and put away. The world isn't going to stop if you're off the airwaves for a couple or three hours.

Some people say that they like to take their own notes at meetings and want, in this high tech world, to do it on their laptop, Notebook, netbook, i-pad or whatever. Fine, but unless you are a copy typist you are probably going to spend more time concentrating on your typing than you are on the meeting that you are being paid to contribute to. And you will be a distraction to others; even if you are not doing your emails they will probably suspect that you are and they will not be paying full attention to the meeting either.

So show some respect and put the electronic devices away. If you must take notes, then take manuscript notes, it's a good discipline anyway, and you can type them up away from the meeting if you have to.

Using an electronic device in a meeting is about you, but the meeting is about a team outcome. If everyone at the meeting is focused on the meeting and delivering a successful outcome then it has a fighting chance of being a success; if it is a group of self-centred individuals then it will probably just waste everyone's time, and that includes yours.

The Universe Conspires to Make it Happen: Oh No it Doesn't

Once you make a decision, the universe conspires to make it happen ~ Ralph Waldo Emerson

I've seen this quote doing the rounds on Twitter, LinkedIn etc and, whilst I understand (I think) what the guy meant, in business practice life just isn't just like that.

The problem is that too many business leaders think that it is; all they have to do is make a decision and, by some form of osmosis, it will just happen. Wrong! Wrong! Wrong!

Yes, making a decision may not be easy, but just making one isn't enough. You have to have a plan to make it happen and that means talking to people and getting them onside. You have to talk to people to motivate and enthuse them to get the job done. You have to empower people to act on your behalf. You have to set milestones and monitor progress. All of that takes communication and action; that's what good leaders are all about and the experience of doing it often enough tends to develop great leaders.

One of the most frequent issues that come from business meetings is that people seem to think that they have agreed to a course of action, but nothing comes of it. Those at the meeting seem to be devotees of Mr Emerson's doctrine.

What needs to happen at any meeting is that any decisions need to be followed up by an agreement on who is going to do what and by when to make them happen. If you don't do that then you are at the mercy of the winds as far as seeing your decision come to fruition.

I earn my crust from helping people move from following the opening quote to making things happen. So sorry RWE, it may be a fine quote and may have some impeccable logic behind it, but from a practical business point of view, it doesn't cut it.

Make your decision and then decide who, how and when it will be implemented before you move on to the next topic. If you do that consistently then your business will probably make some progress. It's what your team will thrive on.

So You're Going to Have a Meeting?

You will, I hope, have prepared an agenda, thought about who will attend, sent out the invitations, the agenda and any relevant papers a sufficient time in advance to allow those attending to prepare, and have booked a room. That sounds right doesn't it? It's what we talked about in Making Meetings Matter.

Well it is good, but what about that last item, the room? How often do you think about that beyond making sure that it is big enough for the number of people who will come?

The quality of the space that you will use for your meeting plays a big part in the quality of the outcome. Sure you can have a quick meeting standing up somewhere; that is actually a very valid solution in the right context, but if you are having a planning meeting, discussing strategy or making an important decision then you need to make sure that the people attending can be comfortable and have all the relevant space and tools that they need.

Let me share with you one of the worst examples that I have come across: We were bidding to win the outsourcing of a service for an international business. On offer was a 3 year deal with options for extension, but the basic contract was worth around £5m. We were invited to present for 40 minutes plus 20 for questions, told we could bring 4 people and use an SVGA presenter. All pretty standard for such a session and we turned up prepared and rehearsed.

We were taken up to the room on an upper floor and on the corner of the building. As the door opened we could see that it was long and narrow. Three tables were end to end down the middle with 6 chairs either side and one at each end, and 11 of these were occupied. The door was in one of the short walls and one long wall and the short wall opposite the door were windows through which the low winter sun streamed.

So basic math will show that there weren't enough seats, and common sense will tell you that we couldn't project onto the door with any degree of success and to project on to the one possible wall meant that half the people would have to turn around and, in any case, the sunlight would wash out the slides.

As Bid Director I had covered for not being able to run the presentation; it's always a risk, so you prepare for it. I'm also used to standing to present, so standing against the door for the hour that we were there was not really an issue even if it was unusual. As for the outcome, well, we got into the final two, so we did OK in difficult circumstances, but what was the point in making use of such a room for the buying team? The people facing the windows were covering their eyes a lot of the time to avoid being blinded and the solar gain was making the room like a sweatbox. We were only there for an hour, but they had five presentations to sit through and debate on, and I would question the quality of the decision making under such conditions of discomfort.

As my Wiltshire colleague Roland Millward points out, so many meeting rooms get used as overflow storage and he asks "Would you hold a meeting in a broom cupboard?" Logic says you wouldn't, but so many people do.

In business you are going to have important meetings, so have a decent space in which to hold them. People need comfortable chairs, they need space to move around in, there should be provision for working in smaller groups, maybe in the room or in nearby breakout areas. There should be provision for flip charts, hanging up flip chart sheets around the walls, proper projection and audio facilities, including decent black out curtains, and the room should be kept clean and tidy.

If you want quality decisions then provide a quality environment for people to work in and make those decisions. One of the ironies is that it costs no more to do it right than it does to do it wrong, so you really have no excuse.

The Meeting Year

In most organisations there will be regular series of meetings and these will often be monthly. Whether you are the main board or one of the functional teams there will probably be a need to gather once a month and chew the fat.
Now all too often these meetings become so routine that they cease to be effective; more or less everyone turns up and goes through the motions of reporting on where they are and maybe makes an excuse for why they aren't where they should be. There is nearly always a standard agenda that takes up the full allotted time, but during AOB the chair will announce that next month you will have to look at budgets, or headcount or something that is going to have to be wedged into the schedule. You probably go to at least one of these yourselves, right?

But how do you break out of this loop? One answer is to have a calendar that sets certain agenda items for specific meetings. Say that your business financial year runs from April to March, in which case you could set quarterly agenda items for July to review the first quarter numbers, October for the second quarter and January for the third. In March you'll be reviewing the outline year end numbers anyway. Sometime between August and October you'll need to set your next year budgets and be looking at things like possible capital projects for the next year. Depending on where you are in the hierarchy you could also look at reviewing how things are going with delivering strategic projects in, say, June, September and December.

There are all sorts of things that need to be discussed and decisions made that you can formally plug into a structured programme so that people know what to expect and prepare for; not just those attending the meeting, but others who will want to contribute ideas or will be affected by the outcomes. This sort of forward thinking means that you can allow adequate time in the meeting for the important issues. Dealing with them in a way that allows the right level of time and discussion, let alone pre-meeting research and planning, is a positive motivator for those that will attend and also provides impetus to your business, or team. If meetings become meaningful through having the right agenda then people will want to come and to participate.

Within this calendar there is the need to have flexibility around how long each meeting will last, and having a varied, agenda for each month leads to variety in duration. Some months you might only need a couple of hours, other months it might be all day, but the key is to schedule enough time for the agenda in each month. Don't allow yourself to set a meeting duration and then try to fill it, and remember that it is as much of a crime to finish early as it is to overrun.

It may well be that you want to take some of these topics outside of the regular meeting and have a separate session. That is fine, but do think hard about why you want to do that because it often isn't necessary and all you do is, once again, allow the subject to fill the time. If people are performing as they should be within their respective functions and you are sharing the information as part of the daily job, then the regular meeting should be the place to be able to discuss and agree strategic and tactical issues and allocate timetables and responsibilities for delivery.

Who's In Charge Here?

There can only be one person in charge at a meeting. Normally this isn't too much of a problem in theory as the person who called the meeting will normally chair it in a multi-function meeting, or the boss in a team meeting, but there is scope for things to go wrong.

In a multi-function meeting there may be issues about who should chair, but this really needs to be resolved before the meeting and not during it. Sort out issues behind closed doors and then close ranks around the decision.
The other time things can go awry is where you bring in an outsider as facilitator. This is a good idea for things like strategy sessions as the facilitator will be someone who is well versed in helping the meeting along towards a positive outcome, but if you do bring someone in then you have to accept that they will be running the meeting.

If there is a need for the MD or other senior person to have some input into the running of the meeting, rather than them contributing to it, then this should be something that gets dealt with between them and the facilitator outside of the meeting. Let everyone take five while you resolve whatever the point is and then carry on. Whatever you do, don't undermine the authority of the person running the session.

To Cater, or Not to Cater?

Budgetary considerations can play a part here, but my basic rule is that if we have holding a meeting of a couple of hours or less and everyone attending works in that building then I probably would not lay on refreshments.

There ought to be a water cooler in the room, and everyone is close to their own preferred source of refreshment; they can bring one with them if they want to and they won't be far from one when the meeting is over.

Longer duration meetings, say half a day upwards I will always have refreshments provided. It is about comfort and looking after the welfare of those there so that they remain productive. And talking about looking after people, if those attending have travelled to the meeting then I will always make sure that they get chance to use the restrooms before the meeting, get them a drink and see that they are looked after before they leave. These basic courtesies are often overlooked and that is a poor show.

If people are travelling to a meeting and will be there over lunch I will feed them, or if the meeting starts or ends around lunch time, I will always make the offer. Again these are basic courtesies.

Chapter Six - Lousy Leaders

Most of these thoughts and stories in this book focus on doing it right, but we can often learn more from things going wrong and from bad examples. Getting it wrong and making mistakes is the most powerful learning zone, so here we look at some bad examples.

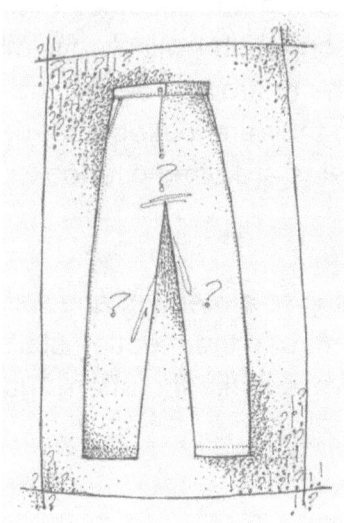

Fear in the Workplace and How to Tackle It

Fear in the workplace is a strong challenge to your leadership skills. It will come as a result of various factors, and defeating it takes courage as well as skill. To begin you need to be listening and watching. Very often people will not talk about their fear or the cause of it and you need to work it out for yourself.

Where I've come across this issue in the workplace it has mostly been because of a bully amongst senior management, and their influence has struck fear all down the management chain so that they all work that way. The second area has been weak management who are ignoring a bully somewhere in the team. My first action in either case is to break that chain and isolate the bully. If necessary I will become a barrier to those above me and to hell with the consequences (career inhibiting behaviour as one such boss told me, but he left the company before me).

Once you have the cause isolated or removed you can work on your team. Show them that you believe in them, get them the tools and resources to do their jobs or whatever else needs doing to give people confidence and banish their fear. Most of all, for me, this is about setting the standard in behaviour. No shouting, no tantrums, just a calm presence that sets the tone for overcoming problems and things that go wrong: Fix the problem without blame and recrimination.

If someone has screwed up work out why and help them by changing the process to mitigate the risk if it happens again. Whatever you have to say to that person who screwed up, do it quietly and behind closed doors 1-2-1.

Of course fear may not be a workplace issue. Someone may be unable to perform at work because of fear generation elsewhere, in their home or family life for example. We may be less able to help directly in these circumstances, but you can identify these things and provide support as best as you are able.

Fear in the workplace is an unpleasant topic, but one that we have to face and deal with. If we can do one positive thing, let's all challenge unacceptable behaviour wherever we find it.

My attempts to overcome the behaviour of the particular boss mentioned above gave rise to one of my leadership mottos; The Team Succeeds, Failure is Mine. I'll explain that in greater detail next.

Bullying Bosses Part One

When I wrote about fear in the workplace I promised to provide some further commentary on the background to a motto that appeared over my desk. There were two versions; "The Team Succeeds, Failure is Mine" and "Our successes are the team's, our failures are mine." As I explained, our big boss at the time was a bully, and management by fear was part of life in that outfit which, in turn, engendered open warfare between functions as making sure that someone else was in trouble meant that, at least for an hour or so, you were in the clear.

The big event was the weekly quality of service meeting where we looked at how we were doing servicing 26,000 outlets with over 30,000 product lines. I ran operations and my opposite number ran purchasing and the protocol was that we would each go with our second in command and then the front line manager for each product area would come in turn to do their bit. A small knot would be gathered in the corridor with those waiting being wound up by the ones who had just had their turn.

His office was set out with a conference table attached at right angles to his desk. There was room for 4 or 5 down each side and for one at the far end facing the big cheese. Over my first few meetings it became apparent that purchasing attendance was dictated by whether or not there was praise coming their way. If things were good, only the top trio would be in the room for that product review, but if there was a problem in a product area both the first line supervisor and the buyer concerned would be wheeled in, that latter getting the seat at the end of the table facing the boss man. The story of misery would unfold from their leadership and then there would be a pause while they waited for the pronouncement from behind the desk. The boss would always be looking down at his papers up until this point, often pecking away at his calculator as he played with the numbers before him. Then, as his head began to rise, the purchasing side would all lean back as though to both give him a clear shot at the miscreant facing him down the far end, but also to distance them from any blame.

The junior member would get both barrels and, ritual sacrifice over, the head of purchasing would assure the boss that the problem would be sorted by the following week always assuming, pause for effect, that operations, could do its part.

For us I changed the pattern. When we were in for praise I wouldn't go, or would excuse myself briefly, but would make sure that someone from the front line got to go in and get a pat on the head. Conversely, if we were up for a kicking, I'd take it on my own. Unlike my opposite number, I'd also take the seat nearest the boss and, if trouble started unexpectedly, would lean across the corner of his desk at him to shield any of my team who might have been there at the time.

Like most bullies he did not like being faced down, but, to give him his due, after some one to one discussions on his behaviour he did try to change and, in his next assignment, he was a transformed character.

So from this scenario came the motto. Since then, whenever my teams have had a win, it is theirs to celebrate. If we've screwed up, I own that problem alone.

Bullying by Colleagues and what You and the Boss can do

Your boss should not be allowing any form of bullying or harassment, but that does not mean that the victim has no need to do anything themselves. Most of these problems in the workplace are mind games; they are about power and control and many, as in the case in question, can seem very innocuous from the outside.

This train of thought was prompted in regard of a colleague who has what I call CJ syndrome. For those not familiar with the world of Reggie Perrin, CJ was his boss, and a running gag through the books and TV series went something like; Reggie; "I'll see you at three on Wednesday", CJ; "Fine, Tuesday at ten". Whatever Reggie suggested, CJ would want something different, and the issue I am looking at was about someone who has a similar problem with a colleague who is always changing meeting times for no apparent reason or finding an excuse for wanting them cancelled at the last-minute.

For me this is classic control freak territory and it is being done for no other reason than to have the upper hand. The perpetrator is getting a kick out of being difficult, so what can you do?

Well, as we've established, these things are about control, and part of the problem here is that you are allowing yourself to be a victim of the other person's actions, so be prepared to make a stand. In many of these cases it isn't always easy for the boss to see the problem, so complaining is not always the right answer. If you do the boss has to speak to the other party about the issue and, at that stage, they are establishing both viewpoints, however distorted they may be. Do you want them just to act on hearsay? Well, yes you do, but they shouldn't if they are a half decent boss.

What they might do is to tell you to get everything in writing and copy it to everyone concerned. OK, if it's a direct order then you'll have to do it, but it isn't likely to work. The first problem is that it is you who is doing all the writing and that is a waste of your time as well as everyone else's who has to read what you've written. The second problem is that, if your protagonist is one of those who are really unpleasant they will turn this against you. I've investigated many bullying and harassment cases and can assure you that the really nasty pieces of work love it when their victim gets into putting it all in writing.

No, you are far better off taking the matter on through your normal ways of working. Don't let them divert or distract you because your performance will suffer and then you have another problem with your boss looming. Stick to your own agenda. Arrange the meetings with colleagues and, if your tormentor wants to change things, say no and hold the meeting without them. Yes there will be some issues, but tough it out. It soon becomes apparent that they are a pain and behaviour will change. You will never become pals, but if they know that they can't get under your skin they'll give up on you and try someone else. When you see who that is, help them overcome the problem.

It is difficult when someone is trying to undermine you, but try to fight your own corner. You have friends and family who can help take your mind off these issues and make you feel good. Whatever you do, don't sink to the other person's level; be true to your own standards. Office jerks may seem to do well, but that is an illusion that they like to foster and, while they have you under their thumb, it may look that way to you. Get out from under and you'll see them for what they are, and that is probably the way everyone else sees them as well.

Bullying Bosses Part Two

Developing this theme, the issue for me is about courage and leadership. Bullies play on a lack of courage in their victims to allow them to get away with what they do, but bullies lack courage themselves. A mark of a good leader is courage, and good leaders stamp out bullying where it crops up, but it doesn't often happen in their teams because they engender trust, and that trust removes much of the fear that encourages bullying.

Leadership can be a very lonely place; leadership is about doing the right things even when these are unpopular and that requires courage in your convictions (amongst a lot of other things). It is not a problem for a leader to be afraid, in fact it is a good thing in many ways because it helps understand risk, but you need the courage to overcome that fear. A leader with the courage to see things through will take their people along with them, they will exude confidence that inspires others and they will help develop those people to deliver results, make things happen and make a difference.

Where leaders lack courage they can't inspire their people, but they still need the results, and the only way that they can see to make their people deliver is to make them afraid of failure, to fear the consequences of not making their numbers, and so the bullying tactics ripple down the chain. The only way of breaking that effect is where there is a leader somewhere in the hierarchy that takes a stand, absorbs the pressure from above and fights their corner. It isn't easy, but it is the only way.

At one company I worked for they adopted a by-line for leadership of Challenging Unacceptable Behaviour. Bullies can only operate where they are allowed to get away with it. They work on the principle of isolating people, they divide and conquer, so if those who are being bullied stand up for themselves and unite in opposition, the bullying can be stopped, but there has to be a desire to do it and there has to be courage. It takes guts to stand up to your boss, and more guts still to stand up to boss squared, but nothing will change unless someone does.

Bullying on the front line does go on in some places, but even a half decent front line supervisor can put a stop to that let alone a little peer pressure, providing that the message is clear from the top, and not just in words, but with example and deed to back it up. Good leadership will not tolerate the wrong sort of behaviour partly because it is wrong and partly because it impedes performance. Neither the bully nor their victim will be pulling their weight.

Real Leaders Know Right From Wrong

To set the scene for this piece on the 28th April 2010, Gordon Brown, then Prime Minister of the UK, was campaigning in Rochdale, Greater Manchester, on the run in to the general election scheduled for the following month. His aides had set him up for some vox pops with potential Labour voters and he was wearing a Sky News microphone so that these could be broadcast to show him in a favourable light.

One of these went badly, and GB returned to his car to berate his team without realising that his remarks would be broadcast to the nation. He subsequently made both public and private apologies for his behaviour.

A leader sets a good example to those that follow, so where does that put our political leader, the Prime Minister no less, who made the remarks that were inadvertently broadcast to the nation, accusing his questioner of being bigoted, but was that not just the way he was behaving himself?

We have plenty of leadership issues here, but I'm going to cover first the issue of doing what is right. I'm going back to basics here and I don't care if you think that I, as my former colleague Alan Johnson (*Labour Home Secretary, a former postman and with whom I share both employment and trade union official links*) has said about Gordon Brown, that I'm "not of this time"; like most of my generation I was brought up with a basic understanding of what was right and what was wrong and this is a core value for me.

Once what GB had said was in the public domain he had no option but to apologise, face to face and that is what he did. He did wrong and then he did right, and I'm not going to offer any judgement on sincerity here.

How many of us would have wanted to walk through that front door under those circumstances?

Along with right and wrong another pillar of my youth was the right to free speech. WW2 was a vivid memory when I was born, and the Korean fracas started just after. All of the people I learned from; relatives, neighbours, teachers, clergy and, in those days, the media were all too aware of the sacrifice that so many had made in the defence of freedom and the right to free speech that was implicit in that freedom.

Children are incredibly cruel and use words to hurt much more than they do fists. Growing up the lines about what was right and wrong about what you could and couldn't say gradually came into focus, and what I suppose you could call the verbal bullying that went on we came to understand as not being right. It didn't stop it, but you learned to temper your language or face the consequences, and in those days there were consequences. Physical bullying was the same; those who did it got sorted out one way or another.

But these were all life lessons; life isn't fair and it never will be. What gives us a chance of being fair is our behaviour; we don't need laws as much as basic principles of behaving well towards each other. Leaders should be at the forefront of this, challenging those who do not behave well, but our PM failed himself, and let the rest of us down, by what he said. Free speech is not about making personal remarks as he did, it is about expressing opinions. Critique ideas, not individuals; there is a difference.

Tony Blair and New Labour have steadily eroded our right to free speech in their time in power. They have sought to prevent the expression of views that do not fit with their own opinions.

Heckling also used to be a feature of the election campaign, but New Labour won't have that either and suppress it vigorously. Ask Julian Borthwick*. They have also removed the ability for those who could police the standards through sanctions. We can't discipline anyone effectively, so the level of verbal abuse has increased to a staggering degree. The fact that GB felt comfortable that he make the remarks that he did is an illustration of the sort of dual standards that have characterised modern politics.

Personally I believe that, unlike his predecessor, Gordon Brown is a good man, but one in the wrong job. I don't agree with his policies, but that doesn't mean that I don't see a decent human being caught up in a job that was beyond him and how those pressures can make you do foolish things. That he was caught out by speaking freely himself, I think, is somewhat ironic; to use his terminology, as he was hoisted by his own petard, he himself appeared somewhat bigoted.

*On 2nd May 2010, three days before the general election, Oxford University dean Julian Borthwick was forcibly ejected from a New Labour meeting in Sunderland for heckling Gordon Brown.

Recruiting the Right People is Crucial, So Why Play The Bully When You Interview Them?

One of my daily forays into the depths of cyberspace got me involved in a discussion on interview questions, in particular the topic of interviewers trying to be clever and, as the original thread put it "catch people (candidates) out".

What sparked the discussion was described as the killer question to ask; "What is it that you can bring to this job that no-one else can?" Now first off that is such a basic question to be asking that anyone not doing so should not be interviewing, but worse still, some of the contributors to the debate seriously endorsed creating an adversarial atmosphere as the right way to interview people and to ensure that you got the best from working that way.

To me this sort of thing is, at best, just lazy, but to advocate it? You're not there to prove that you're cleverer than the candidate. To me it is tantamount to bullying and/or harassment. If some people believe that this way of working is acceptable in an interview then do they change their ways when they deal with people back in the office? I doubt it.

Now my take on interviewing, and I did it regularly for over 20 years, was that my job was to create an environment where the candidate could give their best. That isn't to say that I didn't push them and probe their thinking; I did, but I always wanted them to be able to leave the room feeling that they had been challenged, not humiliated.

The recruitment interview needs to be a tough assessment, yes, but that doesn't mean that it is some sort of battle of wits. The whole point of the process is to be able to get the best out of every candidate so that you can make an objective choice. I firmly believe in the old adage about smart people are the ones that hire people who are even smarter.

Success comes from people and people make up teams. Getting the right people for a team is what interviewing is about. Recruiting good people requires objective decisions based on having given candidates the chance to show their best abilities and talents.

It isn't about proving that you are better than the candidate or establishing a dominant position. Playing silly games, trying to trick or catch out people is counterproductive to selecting the right person. Apart from risking not getting the best out of the interviewee you are allowing all sorts of subjective factors into the decision.

Why would you want to create an adversarial atmosphere? By all means ask tough questions and by all means push the candidate to give their best, but to be adversarial for the sake of it? Trying to get as many people as possible leaving the room as gibbering wrecks isn't clever, it is humiliation and that is bullying.

Strong words? Yes. If I was to behave in any sort of routine employment interview, say an annual appraisal or something of that nature, in the way that some of these people purport to be acceptable in a recruitment interview then I would reasonably expect to be challenged. I am appalled when I read about people talking of doing a good cop, bad cop routine in a recruitment interview and believing that it is acceptable. It is not. If you don't know how to interview, then get someone who can; we're not expensive.

I was trained to interview people on a pass or fail course. We were fed students from the local university and filmed conducting the interview. If you got anything wrong your tutor would enter the room and stop proceedings. Whatever the result we would have to sit with our tutor and the other trainees in our syndicate and watch the video tape of the interview critiquing every question; what we asked, how we asked it, how it was answered and how we followed up. This was gruelling training, but a pass gave you a licence to practice, subject to annual review.

If we had attempted anything like what some of the self-styled experts in that internet discussion group were proposing then that licence would have been withdrawn with no prospect of ever being allowed to interview for that company again.

Good leaders don't need to "catch people out"; they know how to let people shine so that they have the best choice for their team, and good leaders know that hiring people who are smarter than they are makes good sense. In any case the interview should be about the candidate, not the interviewer.

Learning Lessons

Just as we can learn more from our mistakes and we can from our successes, there is much to be learned from a boss that can't get it right. It's also possible, albeit often difficult, to help such a leader get better. Just pause for a moment and consider whether or not the poor leader actually knows that they aren't too good at it. If they have the makings of a good leader then they will know, but you can turn a dud leader into a reasonable one.

At one time I was in a team of four who took on the persona of Dumas' Musketeers and did very much live the All For One and One For All motto. Our boss we regarded as our Richelieu. He was a nice enough bloke socially, but at times a swine as a boss. We started to work on him and, to give him credit, he did try to improve under our pressure, but eventually the needs of the organisation provided a change that enabled him to take an early retirement package. You can change some people, so why not try it?

Chapter Seven - Special Service

Whatever your business you need customers, because if you don't have anyone to do things for you don't have a job. So providing a great service level is something that can make your business fly.

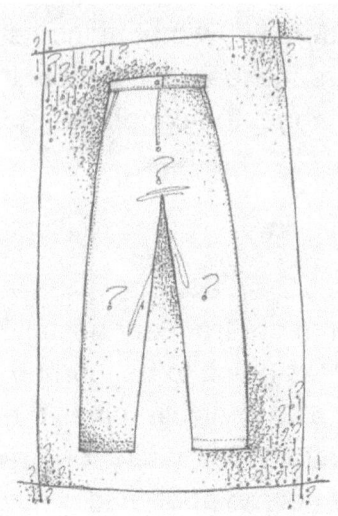

Who is the Most Important Person in Your Company?

It's a pretty straightforward question, so who is the most important person in your business? The boss? The marketing person? Someone on customer service? I won't bore you with a long list here because the answer is a simple one:

Everyone is equally important because any of them can be the difference between success and failure. Even the most humble sounding job needs to be done, and if it isn't done there will be a consequence of some sort.

People work best in a good environment and one of the things that makes people uncomfortable, that distracts them from doing their best, is when the workplace isn't clean. But who keeps it clean? Probably the lowest paid worker on the team, someone who may even be on just the legal minimum wage.

Say you missed out on a piece of business because the person who talked to the customer was distracted by the unpleasant experience of a less than clean office?

Of course there will be certain times when the focus is on an individual to do something special, but to allow that person to concentrate on that special purpose there will be everyone else taking care of things in the background.

How about that easy sale you just made because that customer has never had a problem with any invoice your people have ever sent out?

If you don't want 100% of the people giving 100% effort then why are you in business?

Good results are a team effort.

So next time you are celebrating a good result, don't just reward the person or team that were at the forefront to the exclusion of everyone else; remember that everyone played their part in some way. Success belongs to the team.

Memorable Service, DIY (and could all the world's greatest engineers be women?)

One of my passions is looking at ways that a service can be delivered that will make it memorable, for the right reasons. The crucial element in doing this is in your front line people and the support that they receive through the business, and I argue that this comes more from an attitude than anything else. But to establish the right attitude calls for supporting your team with the right tools and knowledge. Getting this support right, your business processes, is the first step to customer service excellence.

On Saturday I wandered off to the kitchen to knock up dinner for the Berkshire Belle and I. As I assembled various things her melodic voice floated out from the sofa; "Have we got a spare bulb for the light in the cooker hood?"

I'd been putting this off for a few days – FM jobs around the home - and therefore delivering poor service! A good FM would have done it straight away, hopefully before the client saw it, but I've done this job before and it is a swine. You have to get your fingers into a tiny space and do it by feel because your hands are in the way of seeing what you're doing and there is no real room to work in.

Last time I replaced the left side, but this time, with another 3 or 4 years of use, the right one was stuck tight. How to shift it? Dark mutterings weren't helping and brute strength wasn't much use as it would probably break the bulb. Who designed this piece of ****?

Many years ago I came up with the concept that the world's finest engineers were women, and they were secreted away in some James Bond adversary like location, a remote island or deep in the jungle, where they worked away designing flat pack furniture and DIY tasks with deliberate flaws and cruelly misleading instructions with one aim in mind: Reducing men to humiliated, gibbering, wrecks as they struggled to deal with the results of these fiendish minds.

This of course is all just fantasy, however attractive a proposition it might seem. The reason is that things are built down to a price, but the problems are overcome with a bit of ingenuity and acquired knowledge. If you don't know how to fix it you'll hide from it and not do the job if you can avoid it, but if you do know how to do it, and have the tools and skills, it is a breeze.

Back in darkest North Wiltshire I had a flash of inspiration: Dismantle the filters and grease traps and I might be able to get at the bulb that way. Yes, it worked. I had then to clean the stuff I'd removed before reassembling it and dinner was an hour late, but, job done. Client and maintenance man both happy.

Taking this back to the front line, the point I'm trying to illustrate is that if your people don't know how to sort out problems or routine tasks their attitude will be the same as mine was when I noticed that the bulb had failed; it's a problem and it's not easy and I don't want to have to deal with it. Equipping people properly to do their jobs is a crucial element in getting the right attitude to deliver service excellence. Suppliers, is your service product built down to a price or are you equipping your people the right way? Clients, are you scraping the quality off in the name of getting the price down? I know what my choice is.

Make Coming to Work a Pleasure

I watched a TV programme about how children in Hong Kong showed such joy in their understanding of numbers and praised their education and they showed equal joy in going to school and learning. Here I want to translate that into how we, as leaders, educate and equip our people.

When I work with businesses, and when I deal with them as both customer and supplier, the ones that stand out are the ones where the people know what they have to do and have been well trained and equipped to do their jobs. Problems arise when people don't have what they need to do their job. It's pretty obvious really, but so often it happens. The result is demotivated people, dissatisfied customers and lost profit. The fault lies with leadership of course, both for letting it happen and for allowing it to continue.

The baseline solution is to ensure that you have your business processes sorted out, properly documented and rolled out so that people understand how to use them. As an absolute minimum that will get things going in the right direction, but you need to be looking to build on that and take things to a higher level if you want to be making the most of what is your greatest asset; your people.

So what is the difference between the average performance level and moving towards great? It's letting people use their initiative or, to lapse into management speak for a moment, to empower them.

Here we return to one of my regular themes; trust. There has to be a trust between the partners to allow people to use initiative. The boss has to trust the worker to use their initiative wisely and the worker needs to trust their boss not to start shooting if things go wrong.

You start with the requirement that, in any particular process, the worker needs to seek approval from, or to refer an issue to, the next person up in the chain of command. This has to be understood in terms of what it is and why it is there, but also in terms of how often it happens. If you have an area where there is a frequent need to refer, maybe you have a problem in the process anyway and need to review it, but where you have a moderate frequency area, look at giving the worker some latitude. It needs to be talked through to ensure that both sides have grasped the opportunity, but try it. You can always adjust things in the light of experience.

The best examples of this in action are in customer facing roles. Think of your own experience when faced with someone who needs to go and "ask their supervisor". How much more pleasing is it for you if they just say "I can take care of that for you"? And how much more rewarding do you think it is for them? If the problem is a complaint, then it is even better, and not referring the problem up the line avoids that escalation factor that often makes complaints more damaging.

Yes, there are times when allowing people to use their initiative will go wrong and they will overstep the mark, but use this as a learning point. As kids we learn that climbing too far up a tree leads to getting stuck or that the higher you climb, the more it hurts when you fall out. We constantly explore boundaries, so apply that principle here. If someone goes too far in trying to do right it should not be a problem, work on it and learn. Make coming to work a pleasure.

Pay up Promptly, It's Good Business Sense

I was dismayed to read that a certain global brand was pushing its payment terms out to a staggering 65 days

OK, I accept that this is only for certain service lines and doesn't include component supply, but it is still a shoddy move and one that smacks of short term thinking and action that could lead to long term problems.

I am a customer of the company concerned and, in recent weeks, have been looking at buying from them again on two continents. They deliver what I've ordered on time and to specification, and their prices are OK, so I was fairly happy about going back to them again, both here and in the USA.

Supply chains are in fact more of a mesh, and being part of a supply mesh is just that; you are all linked. Yes you can break and replace a link, but, as a mesh, you become an entity and should behave with common interest. Any company can have a short term problem, and neighbouring links in the mesh will often be flexible with each other to share the load for the good of the whole. But that is a different argument to one link in the mesh deliberately passing load to other links. In that circumstance one of the overloaded links is almost guaranteed to fail and a hole appears that, in turn, overloads other neighbouring areas. As things go wrong, confidence in the mesh starts to fail. Other links fail and some decide to leave.

I say that this is short term thinking. Think of your own domestic outgoings. What If you decided not to pay any bills for the next month? Say that saved you two thousand pounds, but the next month you have to start paying your two thousand pounds again. There is no long term saving; you had an extra couple of grand for a few weeks, but now you're back on the same level of outgoings and your debt level has gone up. If it helped you around a problem and you can put some effort into slowly catching up then that's not so much of an issue, but just taking a payment holiday? No; not a good idea.

Times are hard at the moment, and there are two ways that we will get back to better times. One is innovation; being different about how we do things and the offerings that we take to market. The other is through collaboration, working together and looking after each other. I'm not talking about doing away with competition, I'm encouraging it, but there is a need for businesses to help each other where they can work together in serving the market. Where the relationship is contractual then delivering on time on the one hand and paying promptly one the other are crucial elements in making things work.

This is an often overlooked element of Corporate Social Responsibility (CSR). Businesses need each other as much as communities do to provide the means and the way that the individual members of the community can support themselves. I talked earlier about supply chains being a mesh, but that applies to society as well. If businesses truly recognise CSR, rather than just ticking the box, then they have to behave in a responsible manner within their business and local communities.

I cannot believe that the company whose payment policy started this thread here really need 65 day terms. They may not need the thousand pounds I was about to pay them either, but they won't be getting it now. A small protest at their actions perhaps, but their behaviour has offended me.

Delivering great customer service can involve a lot more than just the customer transaction, because if you behave in a way that puts the customer off then they just will not come to you. In this case it will be a long time before I, or my business, spend any more money with this outfit.

What Does Value Mean To You?

Giving value is what all of us in business are, or at least should, be all out, but what is value? The basic answer is that it is what the customer is prepared to pay, and it is a very subjective issue.

What started me off on this train of thought was a stop off at one of my local auctioneers. Over the years I have traded in all sorts of things, both buying and selling at auction, and it does heighten one's sense of value when it is your own hard earned cash that you are speculating with.

I started my professional buying career back in 1971 in the automotive sector, and my goal was the simple one of making a minimum profit on special order items that I would source for customers. As long as I could get what the customer wanted, by when they wanted it, and turn the required profit my boss would be happy and, as we all learn, a happy boss makes for a happy worker.

Buying and selling product is not that different from buying and selling service. On the one side you have an understanding of what your service costs and how much you need to sell it for, and on the buying side you understand your need (or want) and how much you can afford to pay. These are the hard numbers, but there are all sorts of subjective issues that influence the decision.

Both sides can often display an immense degree of arrogance here, and the old adage about people buying people is always a factor, even if one side manages to ignore it in the interests of commercial sense.

Personally I quite like buying from people that I don't like because I know that I have removed the risk of buying because I do like them, and that I might have allowed that fact to colour my judgement about what I was buying and how much I'm paying. And you can extend this personal factor to companies. Some businesses want the cachet of working with big name businesses because it rubs off on sales for both parties.

This is one of the key factors that makes up the difference between cost and price (and vice versa): What is the value that I put on the transaction? If selling I might be influenced by what it would be worth to have a market leading company using my offering. Would that bring other A list customers? As a buyer, would your offering influence my customers in a positive way and help raise my sales?

When I go out to do a supplier appraisal I want to see the operation, and all of it. What is the atmosphere in the workplace? Do the people look effective? Is the place tidy or a shambles? What equipment and systems are being used? All of this will tell me more than reports and presentations ever could and help me make a decision about the value of dealing with these people because I'm far more likely to want to deal with someone who spends their money wisely and runs a tight ship.

Somewhere in the mix between the price you pay and what the cost to you will be is what defines the value.

When all is said and done it is what the consumer is prepared to pay that defines the value. If you lose sight of that you have a problem.

Could You Recognise a Customer if You Saw One?

The central theme to the work I do with clients is around the link between profit, the reason that they are in business, and one source of that profit, the customer. If you can understand how to make that link work then, whilst there are other things that you need to do, you are on the right path.

How you treat your customers, and potential customers, is therefore crucial to business success. Yes, of course this is obvious, and you probably have a mission statement that puts the customer at the heart of what you do, but are you really walking the talk?

How do you recognise someone as a customer? If you run a shop and someone approaches your counter with an item in one hand and plastic or cash in the other then you're going to pretty sure, but for many businesses it is less clear, regardless of whether you are in B2B or B2C. In essence anyone could be a customer or someone with sufficient influence to decide whether or not they or their business are going to trade with you.

As my regular readers will know I am a big fan of going back to the floor. These days I do it just for fun sometimes, but there is a serious purpose to it in terms of understanding how a business really serves its customers.

When I need work done on my car I have used a couple of local garages. Last week I spent a day out for a client delivering car parts to look at some of the coalface realities of achieving their target of delivery within an hour of ordering. As far as the customers were concerned I was just a new face in a familiar van.

Two of those customers were the garages I use to work on my car, and one of them has crossed themselves off my list. Now I don't expect people to recognise the big ugly bloke in tee shirt and jeans driving the parts van as the big ugly bloke in a nice blazer and slacks with the Jaguar who pays them huge sums of money a couple of times a year, but why treat one with utter contempt and the other with a modicum of civility?

I have a very thick skin, but if both management and workers are prepared to be unprofessional and deliberately obtuse with me as a supplier how can I trust their work? Why on earth would I want to remain as a customer when I have plenty of choice elsewhere?

The Environment is a big part of the Corporate Social Responsibility (CSR) agenda, but what do we mean with that E word? Think about the environment in which you trade, your marketplace, for a moment. It may be a geographic community, or a business community, but how are you seen by that community? Your marketing team will be working their socks off on PR and advertising and such, but there's more to it than that.

How do you behave in your community? Respect is a somewhat devalued word these days, but you can start by treating that community with respect. Anybody could be a customer, so treat them as you would like to be treated yourself.

As my friend Ian Berry puts it "My best advice to anyone who wants to significantly improve their performance is - change what's normal." Treat your neighbours and suppliers with the same respect that you would your customers. Why not make all contact with your business a memorably pleasurable experience. Doing good is good for business.

Chapter Eight - Pivotal Points

Throughout my like there have been moments when my life has changed. I didn't always recognise the significance of these events at the time, but sometimes it is only when you reflect that you see these moments for what they are. At other times it is so obvious that you almost have an out of body experience. Here are a few of mine.

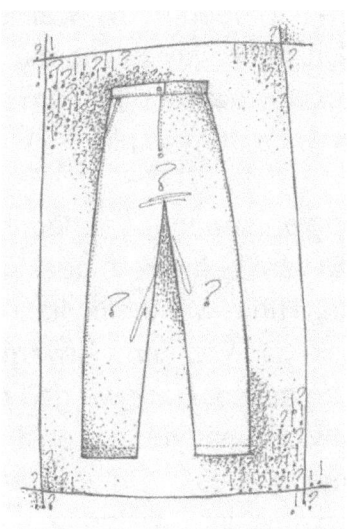

First Steps - Romford, Essex, UK, May 1972 – Being Given A Chance

He stood for a moment before the office door. A tall, gangling and spotty young man dressed in a dust stained warehouse coat.

At one end of him black and white baseball boots peeked from beneath the red velvet bell bottom trousers and at the other end a mop of wavy brown hair sprang from a centre parting to cloak his shoulders.

No-one had told him why he was summoned to see the boss. He was at the end of his fifth week at the firm, his probationary week having proved satisfactory he had been told that he was on an eight week trial, but, despite being promoted the previous week, there had been a few, well issues, so was his trial about to end? Only one way to find out, so he straightened his back, took a pace forward and knocked. "Enter" rang out the voice from within.

I (for I was that spotty personage) opened the door and stepped in. Mr Gibson sat behind his desk, a small, neat man in a small neat office. There was no invitation to sit and so I stood before his desk. "Do you know how much it costs me to employ you here?" he asked. Here we go I though, the sack beckons. "Roughly twice what you get paid" he continued without waiting for me to guess. "Do you understand what net profit is?" he went on, this time raising an eyebrow and pausing for a reply. "It's what's left when you take all of your expenses away from your income" I told him. "So knowing a little of debit and credit columns, if we consider your personal account here in the few weeks that you have been with us you will be aware that there are three significant debits, each of which alone would give good grounds for ending your employment, and a number of smaller withdrawals. Given that you started with a nil balance you could appear somewhat in the red." He paused, but the expression on his face suggested that this was not a moment to interrupt. It wasn't.

"There is an undercurrent of irresponsible behaviour here that cannot be allowed to continue, let alone develop, and it is your good fortune that there have been some credits to your account. There has been an improvement in the figures for your department in the short time that you have been with us and this has been attributed, in part, to your contribution. It is by no means sufficient to wipe out the deficit that your failures have generated, but you have shown signs that you might have the potential to become an asset. You are aware of our management training scheme?"

"Yes Mr Gibson" it came out as barely a croak. "Good. You will be aware then that you do not meet the educational criteria to have entered it, but I do have the discretion to recommend a candidate under exceptional circumstances. Your suggestion for re-laying the stock was adopted and has shown an immediate impact and your general attitude and commitment have made a good impression with a number of my managers. I have been handed the dilemma of whether to dismiss you, retain you or to recommend you for placement on our management training ladder. If I were to put you forward for our management scheme, what could you offer me?"
I began to mumble a few platitudes, but he waved his hand impatiently. "My reputation is at stake here Bowen. See Mrs Frobisher on your way out. She has some papers for you. Take them home, read them, discuss the matter with your parents and see Mr Hopkins (my immediate boss) in the morning. You are an exceptionally lucky young man to have people put their faith in you. Never forget that".

The interview was over. I thanked him and left. Mrs Frobisher was in her cubby hole outside of the office. Without comment she handed me a large envelope with my name on the front. When I opened it in the privacy of the Gents toilet a few moments later I found it to be a new contract of employment as a management trainee.

Did I accept it? You bet I did. Did I blow my chance? You bet I did. I was to let my own sense of self importance outstrip reality and walk out on the opportunity two and a half years later only to find that I had make a dreadful mistake.

Did I waste the chance? Not entirely, because what they gave me in that two and a half years was a foundation that I was later to build on, but youth, immaturity, inexperience, arrogance, stupidity and ignorance all had to be worked through my system before I woke up to what I could achieve, and it was only a happy accident that opened the right door to give me another chance.

Taking Responsibility For Your Own Actions

Sometimes an innocent question can cause you to take a fresh look at something that maybe you had closed your mind to.

"So you mean, like, a risk assessment? " Out of the mouths of babes and innocents, as they say. The teenage young lady who had asked me that waited for me to respond, but with no concept of the pennies that were dropping for me.

I'd picked up a voicemail the previous week from a journalist acquaintance. Could I write a short piece and then do an interview based on it she had asked. Of course I could, and a contribution to the Florida fund sounded possible as I rang back, but what she wanted was for me to help her daughter with a school project on how teenagers had coped in previous decades. So I signed up for an unpaid assignment, wrote what turned out to be a couple of thousand words and then met the two ladies in the local Starbucks to answer some questions.

We talked about school, homework and exams, about uniforms, music and all sorts of things, my world being as alien to her as hers is to me. How we coped without modern technology seemed to fascinate her. When I told her that, for much of my teenage years we didn't even have a phone at home it strained her credulity; how could we survive without a phone?

The lack of computer games was another gulf. What did we do? Well, we pretended. Her eyes were out on stalks as I told her that we would see a film or TV programme and just playact stuff. The same with books: Lord of the Rings for example was one fad, and we just played the parts and made out that the local recreation ground was middle earth or whatever. Adopting a character in your mind isn't that different from adopting it through a PC or console after all.

But then she asked the killer question: How often did we get into trouble and what happened when we did? When I told her that we might get a walloping off the local copper! Police brutality! And that I'd not tell my parents for fear of further sanctions, as opposed to them rushing to the police complaints team.

It was at the point where I told her that we would balance the thrill, or whatever, of doing something wrong against the likelihood of getting caught, and then if we got caught, what the punishment might be, that she came up with the phrase that stopped me dead; "So you mean, like, a risk assessment?"

It is exactly what I meant, but it had never occurred to me that that was what it was until she suggested it. I have blogged about how old things get re-floated as the Next Big Thing, and here was another classic case, albeit that I had never thought of it that way before.

So yes, as kids we did carry out a sort of mental risk assessment: What were the chances we'd get found out? If so, what would the consequences be? Humiliation, pain, loss of privileges, a good hiding, several good hidings? Was it, therefore, a risk worth taking? There were, of course, the times when you were too far down the road before you thought of any of this – may as well be hung for a sheep as a lamb.

The difference is that there was the element of personal responsibility. We accepted that it was our decision. We learned to understood about personal responsibility: This looks like good fun, but I might have to pay for it later.

Somewhere along the way efforts to remove risk and danger from our lives seem to have stopped us learning these lessons and these days people just seem to want to be victims, blaming everyone else for any misfortune that comes their way.

Second Steps – Romford, Essex, UK, August 1976 – From The Bottom Again

I locked the shop door and turned the sign to closed. The Senior Engineer and I walked back through the shop checking that everything that should be off was and locking up behind us. Having set the alarms we closed and locked the back door and I handed him the keys. My tenure as holiday relief manager at one of the region's two flagship stores was over. "Well done kid" he said and thumped me on the shoulder. I thanked him and we drove off in our company branded Ford Escorts.

It was two years almost to the day since I had left that shop through the front door out into the shopping mall having been hired as a salesman/installer by the man whose holiday I had just relieved. I had served a 3 week apprenticeship there before being allocated to the Dagenham shop where I spend the next 18 months making a name, of some sort, for myself. I made enough of a name to be moved to work out of a pair of showrooms on the wealthy Eastern edge of our region where my earnings soared.

When we left First Steps I had walked out on a management training scheme. I had done so on the cusp of taking over a department at the age of 22, a good 10 years younger than any other department manager at that branch depot. I had left to follow the lure of going on the road as a salesman which, under normal circumstances, I would have spent 6 months doing on the management training scheme.
But I was impatient and, when I had asked when my time on the road would come, I was told that I was not considered to be sales representative material and that they believed it would be a waste to send me out as one.

Instead I would short circuit the process and, in 2 to 3 months, take over the automotive paints department when the current incumbent moved on.

Instead of accepting this golden opportunity I saw only the negative of being turned down for a sales rep job. On the bus home that night I looked at the job ads in the local paper. One for a sales rep at another motor factor caught my eye and, the next morning, I walked up to the call box and rang them. The boss was there and I was put through. "You're advertising for me in the paper, when can I come and see you?" I asked, with all the bravado I could manage. "How about now?" was the answer and half an hour later I was on my way out of his office in Rainham ready to start a week Monday.

I gave my seven days' notice and stuck to my guns despite every effort being made to talk me out of it and started work at my new job. It went wrong from the start; they had no vehicle for me for nearly three weeks, but I learned the stock and the ropes as best as I could and learned all of the workshop jobs to boot. My company car turned out to be a company van, but never mind; I was on the road around the East End of London selling commercial vehicle spares and hydraulic fittings. I was a Rep!

Problems continued though. My first month's figures were in, but instead of setting me a target based on them my area got changed a little, then the same the next month, then the guy who worked South of the river went sick and I was sent to cover him for nearly a month, then I came back to find that they had hired my rival from a competitor and given him my prime area.

My new car turned out to be a 5 year old and well worn one and I could never earn commission because they kept changing the rules. Oh, and there was woman trouble too; never have an office romance they say, but I'd add never have an office romance with the one that the boss fancies, but can't get anywhere with.

The local paper came to my rescue again with the job as a salesman and installer for a TV rental company. My visit to their shop in Romford landed me the position and I thrived. Two years on from joining them I was being viewed as one of the two best in our job on the region, and then the other guy became my boss when that job came up for grabs.
Again I was gutted, but I had matured some by then. Ted was a good boss. He knew and understood how I felt and never once was less than encouraging and supportive. Twenty years older than me he was another Father figure to a degree and helped open the door for me to join the relief shop manager panel with the result that I was straight off to Romford as we saw at the start of this story.

My time with this company was limited, although I didn't know it at that point. I was to get engaged soon afterwards and the problems of being able to afford a home came into the equation. I worked 6 days a week, giving up my day off to earn money, and worked from 0800 in the morning until 8 or 9 at night. All of this meant that I had little time to myself, but living in the middle of my working area meant that I could pop home, run errands and fit things in whilst taking home around 4 times my basic salary.

Buying a house that I could afford meant moving 25 miles or more away. A transfer to the appropriate region was offered, but it meant starting at the bottom again and my commission earnings in a rural area would be tiny compared to those from suburbia and so a change of job was called for.

A brief interlude as a driving instructor came to an end when I was able to join the Post Office as a counter clerk. The pay was grim compared to what had been earning in the TV rental business, but was more consistent than that as a driving instructor and the hours were much more conducive to the DIY needs of an old Victorian semi-detached house owner. I joined, and it would be almost 31 years before I left (ignoring various departmental moves and being transferred to a joint venture business).

Having learned from past mistakes I had made a sound career move into another business where I had prospects. I knew it not at the time, but, with some sound foundations in place at last, at 26 I had taken what would be the final step towards a concerted assault on the greasy pole of management.

Oh, and within about 4 years the TV rental business was showing signs of decline. I got off that bus at just the right time, even if I didn't know it when I made the choice.

You can be Pat the Cleaner – A Lesson in Humility

It was late in 1973 and I was days from my 21st birthday. Eighteen months or so earlier I had landed a job as a store man/counter hand for a much loved national wholesale company and had done well enough to be promoted to stock controller within a month and then allowed to join the management trainee scheme after all.

The management training ladder decreed that you had to spend time in every department and I had fast tracked my way round making improvements of some sort everywhere I went. Life was good and I was impatient, more so because I seemed to have stalled with only a spell on the sales team to add to make my experience sheet complete. I had to be 21 to be allocated a company car and that milestone was close, so I asked to see the depot manager.

Mr Gibson sat behind his polished desk with its leather inlay. "Well Bowen?" he asked. I put my impassioned case to gain that one last piece of experience that would, assuming that I didn't screw it up, would allow my name to go forward to the panel of prospective future managers. I stood before his desk as we talked about what I had achieved, he tempering my trumpeting with some sharp reminders of my foul ups (including my reversing a van into his car whilst chatting up one of the office girls).

Then what I had come to know as a twinkle came into his eye. "Bowen. You may be able to help me solve a problem" he said and picked up the phone. The one side of the conversation that I could hear made no sense, but he was obviously satisfied as he put down the phone. Was he lending me to another depot? That would be a real opportunity.
He regarded me for a moment before speaking. "Well Bowen, I think I have the perfect change of scenery for you. A vital job and something very different for you to add to your repertoire. Pat the cleaner is going on holiday for the next two weeks. You will be Pat the cleaner while she is away. That's all".
I tossed and turned that night and seriously considered just not going back. I was a hot shot, fast track, management trainee that surely someone else would value. Why should I put up with being a cleaner?

The next day I did turn up and was released from my normal job to understudy Pat. She had me sussed out and knew just what buttons to press. By the end of the day I was determined that she would come back to a palace.

The two weeks flew by. I cleaned surfaces horizontal and vertical. I hoovered and I mopped. I polished the brass fittings and Mr Gibson's desk. I scrubbed the toilets and the washrooms. There were some real positives; by the end of the fortnight I knew everyone in the building and they knew me and, thanks to the graffiti in the Ladies restrooms, I knew things about my mates that they would rather I kept to myself (I was not sure whether to be delighted or disappointed that I barely rated a mention).

Most of all I had been given a lesson in humility and, although I didn't know it then, taken a first step towards, many years later, becoming a facilities manager.

Chapter Nine - Simply Stories

We talk a lot in business these days about having a story to tell. We also talk, within leadership circles, about opening yourself up and showing some vulnerability. So here I share some personal stories that will help put into context some of my thinking and the things that have helped to shape me.

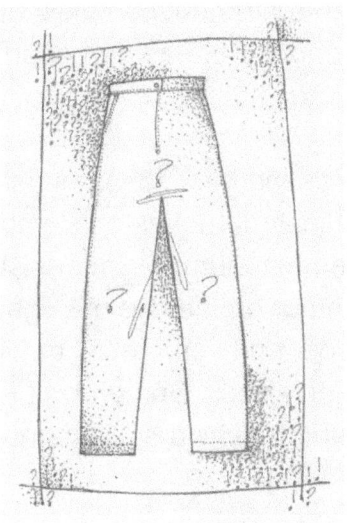

Going Round In Circles

I wrote this next story at a busy time in the life of That Consultant Bloke. In late 2010 we were starting a new, fairly long term, project for an equally new client and there was a lot to do as you try to get under the skin of the thing, then there was getting a new office organised as we tried to build our business infrastructure in line with our order book and plans. Both of these had led me full circle in some way or other.

On the office front we have established a foothold 25 miles or so to the south west in Newbury. I guess I should have short cut the decision making process as the new base has the post code suffix 1JB. That alone should have settled it, but I didn't notice until I was signing the papers. A Newbury base takes me back to where it all started for me nearly 60 years ago as it is my home town. My arrival at Sandleford Hospital isn't marked by a blue plaque; they tore the place down a few years ago to build an apartment complex, but it's a good feeling to have a toehold there as part of an expansion to the business.

The new project takes me back to, amongst other places, Portsmouth. My earliest memories on Pompey are from way back in the 50s when my Mum, younger sister and I had a 2 week holiday at Ventnor on the Isle of Wight. Dad couldn't come because of work and I can recall getting a bit tearful as we sailed from the ferry dock. Somehow it felt like we were really leaving something behind as Portsmouth Harbour receded.

About 10 years later I was back for a 3 week stay in the summer of love as a 14 year old experiencing relative freedom for the first time and an explosion of hormones. We stayed next door to Portsmouth in Southsea, but I explored all over and grew to love the place as, with the sun and the music, it provided a backdrop to my growing up.

Scroll forward another 14 years or so and I was there again, twice as old, but this time working there for just over 2 years and travelling home to darkest north Essex at the weekends.

This was the project that launched my business career, saw my ugly mug featured on the national TV news, brought me into contact with the great (and good?) and established my reputation for making things happen. My time there changed my life in more than one way and left me with a host of skills as well as some fantastic memories. If I have to pick one it would be when the salvage ship Tog Mor inched the Mary Rose clear of the Solent waters. I've always had a soft spot for history and to have been there when that relic of Henry VIII's time returned to reveal her secrets was truly special.

I've been back to Portsmouth and Southsea for all sorts of things since, but the prospects of making it a regular haunt again for the next year or so fills me with a sense of excitement. The place has featured so much in getting me to where I am today, making me the man I am today, that I feel a debt of gratitude.

It's strange how certain places feature regularly in my life. Like Romford, both Newbury and Portsmouth have a place in my history and my heart, and it's good to be hooking up with both again. Someone once suggested that I was worth hiring because I had "been around the block often enough". Going round in circles works for me; I like to remember my roots.

The Ghent Agenda

I've mentioned the Ghent Agenda elsewhere in this book, but think it is worth telling the full story. The time was the early 90s and I was running a large logistics operation. One facet of that role was Facilities Management so, when it was suggested that I make another trip to the Hannover Messe (trade fair), I decided to take two of my FM team with me.

It was cheaper to drive than to fly so we headed off through the Chunnel and spent a heavy two and a half days pounding the halls before setting off after lunch to return home.

Our plan was to see how far we could get by late afternoon before making the decision on where to stay, and we started to see signs for Brussels around that point. None of us had been there, so we thought we'd give it a try, and I suggested that we follow the signs for the airport as that would give us a range of hotels. Sure enough we found a selection, but car parks were pretty much full. We stopped at the first one that we could park at and I dived out into the rain to try and get us rooms.

At that time I had been working in Germany frequently and was wearing a sports jacket that I had bought on one of my trips there. I also had what the Berkshire Belle refers to as my Herman the German haircut, a number three all over crew cut that she says is a bit Prussian.

I approached a receptionist who was just finishing dealing with an Italian chap (I guessed that he was Italian as that was the language that they were speaking). As he turned away she smiled at me and addressed me in German, presumably because of my general look. I responded in German, asking for three rooms, but she recognised the English accent and switched to my native tongue. She was sorry, but there was a major EU conference in town and all rooms were taken. Where were we headed? I explained that we would be going back to the UK via Eurotunnel the next day and she asked me to wait while she tried to find me something.

In the next couple of minutes I listened to her switching between Walloon and Flemish while she spoke to colleagues in the hotel and on the phone and the outcome of these was the offer of three rooms at their hotel in Ghent, about an hour's drive away, but on our way to Eurotunnel. I accepted the offer, she confirmed the reservation and provided directions and I left impressed and thoughtful.

We found the hotel in Ghent and checked in. As I was concluding the payment there was a commotion from behind and I was swamped by a coach load of Orientals with no concept of taking things in turn. No matter, I extricated myself from their mob and went off to my room. I had just finished unpacking and was contemplating a shower when the phone rang. It was reception to tell me that they had omitted to return my credit card (not that I had forgotten to take it as might normally have been the case) and would it be convenient to bring it to me? I offered to collect it later, but no; it was their error and they wanted to put it right.

The receptionist who had dealt with me was at my door within moments, apologising for having been distracted by the Korean delegation arriving as they had. He asked if my room was acceptable and suggested that if we wished to dine we might prefer to take a stroll around the city centre as the Koreans were about to descend on the hotel restaurant. He suggested a few places we could consider and withdrew.

Showered and changed I re-joined my colleagues and went for a short walk to find one of the recommended restaurants. Over dinner I talked about my experiences at both hotels and we looked at how we could turn our team performance into something as proactive. We wrote out a list of personal and team goals that we called the Ghent Agenda.

At the heart of this was the premise that we should accept that we might not be able to deliver what the client wanted every time, especially when what they wanted was outside of what we were contracted to supply, but that we should not just pass on bad news, shrug and walk away, rather that we should be able to suggest alternatives and try to work towards an acceptable solution.

Implementing these plans was, as always, not as easy as it was to devise them, but we began to try and convince them team that this was a better way of working for them and for our clients.

The Ghent Agenda came about through the experience I encountered in those two hotel receptions in Brussels and Ghent. They crystallised my thinking on customer service and enabled me to articulate it. I've been promoting those principles ever since.

Having Fun and Making Dreams Come True

Social media has put me in touch with many people. Mostly I've made new contacts, but it has also put me back in touch with people from my past and that, in turn, has got me thinking about the fun we had and the dreams we shared back in those carefree days.

Around the time that Neil Armstrong was taking his small step/giant leap onto lunar soil I was doing my own equivalent leaving school for the great wide world. The start of my journey was a village called Cobham in Surrey, on the A3 Portsmouth road just to the south west of London. These days the modern A3 by-passes the village and the M25 has carved through the woods that I played in as a child. So much has changed, yet much is still recognisable. I am over that way quite often on business and sometimes for pleasure. Any trip brings back memories of my teens; a growing interest in girls, becoming conscious of fashion, buying records, paper rounds and Saturday jobs.

I lived there for 5 years from just before my 12th birthday to just before my 17th, so the place had a big influence on some of the most important formative years of my life. When the Apollo astronauts first landed on the moon it was just over 60 years since the first powered flight. Yes that progress had been accelerated by two bloody global conflicts and yes the US rocket programme was based on the Nazi weapons research, but it was still an astonishing rate of progress. In the 40 years since I left Cobham that pace has, if anything got faster.

The mobile/cell phones we have now were mere science fiction then. Even in the early 80s, as a COBOL programmer I was trying to squeeze programmes through 1k of memory during overnight processing. That last sentence would take more now, and to have 8+mb on a phone that fits into my pocket was fantasy.

Not all change suits me, but it has to happen, and somewhere along the way for me it became apparent that I did not have to be a passive force; I could influence change. Partially that comes with where you sit in life. It is a lot easier to shape things from a position of authority and that, in turn, comes from experience and climbing the ladder, but you chose whether you want it or not. If you do want it, and set out to get it, influence will come to you.

I left school with no real ambition. I wanted a job because I had been brought up to know that work equalled money and money bought the things I wanted. At the top of that list was a car and I would dream about driving around the village in something nice, but I had no real idea about what I wanted to do.

Life has been good to me and I've been extraordinarily lucky. From those unfocused beginnings I put together a career that has taken me all round the UK and into Europe. It has put money in my pocket to travel and I have the treasured memories of countless experiences and people. Sure there has been some bad stuff, but I park that and keep the fun. I can't change what has past, only the future.

I drive through Cobham now in my Jaguar, so my dream came true. So much has changed and so have I, but making change happen delivered my dream. And I'm still having fun.

Robert the Bruce Had a Spider; I Have a Tripod Squirrel

I call her my squirrel, but it's really the other way round; I'm her human. I also call her Samantha, but she wouldn't recognise that as her name, albeit it that she does know my voice.

A tripod squirrel? Well she started out with a full complement of legs when I first saw her in our garden about four years ago. She came regularly to share the bird's food and we were happy to accommodate her. One spring she turned up with two youngsters which was great fun for a couple of weeks until she managed to pry loose a piece of the soffit and moved herself and her family into our loft.

That we had to draw the line at because of the risk of fire from gnawed power cables, but the nest she had made was a thing to behold. The sheer strength and willpower it must have taken to have moved some of the material she had found across all the rafters belied belief and I was sad to have to move her out.

She bore no malice though, and continued to come and feed. The children moved on and another winter went by, but then she appeared with what looked like a fabric band aid on the front right foot. I can only suppose that she had been rummaging somewhere and got the foot into a discarded one that had enough adhesive left to stick to her fur. We thought about catching her, but that wasn't a great idea, and the animal rescue people reckoned that they couldn't help as the trauma of being caught would probably kill her. They told us to leave her and it would fall off of its own accord.

She still had it in place through 2008 and it was still there when she re-emerged in 2009. Then she turned up with that leg missing from the elbow; just a bloody stump. We talked to the animal welfare people again and they shared our view that she had bitten off her own forearm but, again, they didn't want to intervene as she appeared, otherwise, to be healthy. Another animal group said they would trap and euthanize her, but we felt she should take her chances.

I've just been talking to her again this morning. She has been for her feed and had taken up station in our cherry tree for a post breakfast ablution. The tip of the stump is bright red where she has taken the scab off, but if you see her from most angles the missing forearm is not noticeable and she looks fine. She shins up trees and the fence with no problem and can even climb a half inch thick metal pole with ease.

Where she lives we don't know, but she we see her often. She has the neighbourhood cats sussed out, including ours, and treats them with casual contempt. She is so much faster than they are and those that have tried, and failed, to lay a paw on her now ignore her too.

One day, of course, like Jackie Paper, she will come no more. She is at least five years old now, possibly six, so we may get another year, who knows? We'll be sad when we get to the stage that we've not seen her for so long that we know she must have met an end. We've loved having her around and, for me, her tenacity has been a true inspiration. Robert the Bruce may have had his spider; I have my Samantha Squirrel. "Never, never, never quit! " – Winston Churchill.

The Joy of Numbers

I watched Griff Rhys-Jones' programme on Hong Kong on TV. Seeing those kids singing mental arithmetic was great, as was the sheer delight on their faces. Teaching kids by these sorts of methods is not so far from the chants that we used when I was in primary school at a similar age, yet such methods are ridiculed by modern teaching experts. If they are right why am I interviewing UK graduates that can't add up? If they can't even do simple stuff with a pencil and paper and a little time to ponder having been taught through our modern education system, how come those Hong Kong kids can do more complex stuff in their heads at lightning speed?

Possibly the answer is in the level of enjoyment. Over the last 30 years I haven't met a product of the UK education system who liked numbers, but the Hong Kong children loved them. I think that the teaching methods have much to do with that. If they work, and you start to understand how numbers work, then you get pleasure from using them. If you don't understand them, they become a barrier and you close your mind.

The children in Hong Kong were mentally visualising an abacus. Yes it is a form of calculator, but it is a manual one, and the problem with an electronic calculator is the one of garbage in, garbage out. With an abacus you can see your mistakes; with a calculator you can't, unless the result is so far out as to be obvious.

This is one of the problems I find with younger colleagues and spreadsheets or computer produced reports. They usually can't see that something is wrong because they don't have enough of a grasp of numbers to be able to tell that there is a problem, other than, maybe, if a month on month graph shows a strange result, but that is the picture, not the number, that shows the error.

Good teaching should be measured by results; have the students learned what they have been taught? From my own experience of the old methods and from what I see of the product of the new methods then I think we are failing horribly. And don't start quoting exam results at me either, because I can't see how someone can have passed A level maths when they can't do basic sums unless standards on pass levels have been lowered dramatically.

Here I go again, but when I was between 19 and 23 I worked a second job in pubs as a barman. In those days we would have to add the rounds up in our heads whilst getting the drinks orders right and watching the bar to work out the right order to serve people in. There was no mercy from the customer if you got the total or the change wrong (for younger readers, in those days you could only key into the till the total price for the round and it didn't tell you what change to give) and the till had to balance to the penny at the end of the shift. On a Friday and Saturday evening some rounds would be 30+ drinks, but we got it right time after time, (as did our customers) because we had all been taught well.

My education was primary school and county secondary modern; just the basic standard, but it did its job and gave me a good platform to go out into the world and learn more.

Children are our future; please let's teach them well, like they do in Hong Kong.

Epilogue

Third Steps, London, February 1982 – Coffee and a Happy Accident

I left my personal journey in Chapter Eight in Second Steps seemingly about to make positive progress and to capitalise on my experiences and so I felt that I should end this book with the story of the happy accident that opened the door for me to get centre stage and make something of all I had learned so far.

Towards the end of 1981 things had got tough. I was getting desperate for a better job as an unplanned, at the time, second child was on the way and we needed more money; at the end of each month I was walking the 8 miles each way to and from the office because I couldn't afford the bus fare let alone petrol or car parking. I had missed out on a local promotion by virtue of having missed the seniority cut off by just 4 days. (You have to draw the line somewhere, but that one hurt). I had applied for the national fast track panel, got through the weeding out and into the last 50, but failed to make it into the top 20. I was looking for a better paid job, but not much was about and my wife and I were sharing two evening cleaning jobs to make ends meet.
It was a sparse Christmas, but the New Year bought a result. The company was ramping up its new computer division and they were looking for internal people with aptitude to augment the outsiders that had been recruited.

I had applied the previous November and got straight through to interview based on my performance in the fast track panel assessments. In that first week of 1982 came news that I had been accepted and was to report to London in early February to take up my new job which was to be part of a major financial systems development team (this was a flagship project; think of a home grown version of SAP).

On the appointed Monday I caught an early train up to Liverpool Street station. I wanted to be sure I was there in good time for my induction and left early on the basis that I could get a breakfast in one of the many local cafes in The City. Once in London I walked through towards the office only for realisation to dawn that I had left my wallet at home; I just had a few coins that might buy me lunch in the subsidised canteen, but breakfast was a non starter. I couldn't even afford a coffee at London prices.

It was freezing and so I decided to go straight to the office to at least get out of the cold. I walked into the same marbled reception that I had been through for my interview a couple of months before and approached the same security guard. He was not sympathetic; "You're too early mate. Sit over there and wait" he said, pointing to a row of basic office chairs against the wall. Oh, well, at least I was out of the bitter chill.

I had barely sat when a voice called my name. It was a good friend of my wife's who also worked in that building. Having established what I was there for she told the guard that she would look after me and took me round to where she worked and made me a coffee.

We swapped stories and she explained that she, too, had joined the computer team and had started a new assignment the week before.

Her project was a small one working on a pilot scheme. The boss was in place as were the 4 team leaders plus her and one other with six more people due to start soon. The bosses were all out on the road seeing suppliers and she and the one other guy were getting the office set up with the basics.

Chatting away time passed and realisation suddenly dawned that I was supposed to have reported nearly an hour since. We rushed to the allotted room to find three ladies starting to pack up. One solitary name badge sat on the table inside the door; it had my name on it.

Apologies and explanations proffered, the three ladies from Personnel were unimpressed, but I was taken first to their office where I waited for a while and then taken along corridors and up stairs to another office. I was ushered in and introduced to a man who was apparently my boss cubed (in hierarchical terms; boss, boss squared, boss cubed).

He was friendly and explained that there were two Bowens due to start that day. As I was apparently not there and the project to which I was assigned was in urgent need of bodies the other Bowen had been given my job and had gone off to start work. Still, he told me, there was some good news in that I would get his job assignment. Instead of being a project co-ordinator I would be going on a three month course in London to train as a computer programmer. Further good news was that my promotion would still take effect from today, but he asked if I could do him a big favour.

The problem was that the job I would be taking was not ready to start and the training course was scheduled for the following Monday. The other Bowen had been sent a letter asking him to delay his arrival for a week, but the letter had apparently gone astray. There was nothing for me to do, so would I mind awfully just going home and coming back next Monday? He'd be obliged if I didn't tell anyone of course.

A week off on full pay, and at the new rate to reflect my new grade I mused as I sat on the almost empty late morning train home. I was disappointed to have missed out on the company's flagship project, but to be trained to programme computers seemed like a win and what was effectively a 20% pay rise was going to help a lot, so go with the flow I thought. That stop for a coffee and a chat had far reaching effects on my career path over the next 5 years: The project that I had originally been assigned to was a nightmare and ground to some sort of a halt with partial implementation, but within 10 years the business bought SAP to replace it.

I joined the lady who had made me that coffee in the gang of thirteen. We had a little government sponsorship for our project and it became the subject of huge focus over the next 18 months. I found myself on first name terms with the Chairman and the MD as well as several other senior figures in the business. I attended meetings in Whitehall, including one chaired by a cabinet minister. I stood 6 foot from the Prime Minister at one gathering and a shot of my boss and I opened the news bulletins on all four TV channels on the lunchtime, early and late evening editions. A reputation as someone who could get things done attached itself to me and it catapulted me up the ladder, but my namesake who had taken my original place vanished without trace in amongst a cast of hundreds on that project; if it hadn't have been for that coffee I would never have got the chance to shine.

Luck plays a big part in life sometimes, but it can be of your own making. It was Gary Player who said that the more he practised the luckier he seemed to get. I had been given chances before by people who saw something in me and pushed me towards success, but I blew those chances. This time the opportunity came by happy accident, but I had learned and matured. Yes I did come near to blowing this one as well, but the accumulated knowledge and experience carried me through. I grabbed my chance and took it.

If there is a moral to this story, I guess that it is that you should always make time to have a coffee with someone when the chance comes; you never know where that caffeine and conversation will take you, but it may be time well invested.

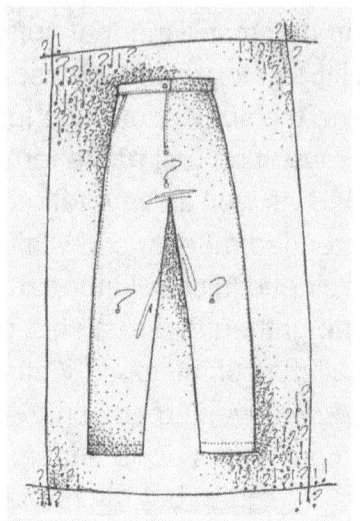

Acknowledgements

I'm grateful to Ian Berry and Kwai Yu for their various support, company and conversation during the time that these thoughts were written. You may well also be inspired by them and you can find out more at:

Ian Berry www.changingwhatsnormal.com
Kwai Yu www.linchpinacademy.org

Bibliography
Last Bus to Albuquerque, Lewis Grizzard, published by Longstreet Press ISBN 978-1563521843 was referred to in Chapter Four

The Fall and Rise of Reginald Perrin, David Nobbs, published by Methuen as part of The Complete Reginald Perrin ISBN 0413638804 was referred to in Chapter Six

Feedback
I welcome your thoughts on any aspect of this book
books@thatconsultantbloke.com
www.thatconsultantbloke.com

About

Back in 2001 a business that the company I worked for did a lot of trade with asked if we could help one of their major clients, a global banking corporation. The bank was planning a move of their London headquarters to a new site and I was roped in to spend a couple of hours going through one aspect of how things would work in the new site.

Their problem was a bit of a specialism for me at the time and I gave advice on the same issue to the Cabinet Office in respect of how things could be improved in that area at 10 Downing Street. I gave the bank the benefit of my knowledge and that, I thought, was that.

About 4 months later the Director at the bank that I had worked with called our friends and asked them to get that consultant bloke back to give advice on another topic. That Consultant Bloke; it went around the office like wildfire and I couldn't escape the nickname for a few weeks before it went out of fashion.

When I left the corporate world in 2008 and set out on my own one of my pals from the old days reminded me of the tag That Consultant Bloke. Running it past a few other pals suggested that it might be worth adopting as a brand and so I did.

I can help you or your business

I provide tailored sessions or workshops for individuals or any size of group to inspire and provoke thought. Please contact me at john@thatconsultantbloke.com and let me know what you need.

I can speak at your conference or seminar

I am very happy to provide a talk or interactive session for conference and seminar organisers. Email me at john@thatconsultantbloke.com to check my availability and start a dialogue about what your audience need to hear.

www.ingramcontent.com/pod-product-compliance
Lightning Source LLC
Chambersburg PA
CBHW051314170526
45166CB00002B/545